Two Years

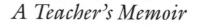

A Teacher's Memoir

Mary Kenner Glover

With a Foreword by
Georgia Heard

Heinemann
Portsmouth, New Hampshire

Heinemann Educational Books, Inc.
361 Hanover Street   Portsmouth, NH 03801-3959
Offices and agents throughout the world

The author and publisher wish to thank the following for permission to reprint previously published material in this book:

Page 49: From *Julie of the Wolves* by Jean Craighead George. Text copyright © 1972 by Jean Craighead George. Reprinted by permission of Harper-Collins Publishers.

Page 78: Reprinted with permission of the publisher from Greene, Maxine, *Landscapes of Learning.* (New York: Teachers College Press, © 1978 by Teachers College, Columbia Unviersity. All rights reserved.), p. 3.

Page 93: Excerpts from *The Little Prince* by Antoine de Saint-Exupery, copyright © 1943 and renewed 1971 by Harcourt Brace Jovanovich, Inc., reprinted by permission of the publisher.

Page 103: Excerpts from *The Writing Life* by Annie Dillard. Copyright © 1989 by Annie Dillard. Reprinted with permission of HarperCollins Publishers, Inc.

Every effort has been made to contact the copyright holders and the children and their parents for permission to reprint borrowed material. We regret any oversights that may have occurred and would be happy to rectify them in future printings of this work.

Library of Congress Cataloging-in-Publication Data
Glover, Mary Kenner.
    Two years : a teacher's memoir / Mary Kenner Glover.
      p.   cm.
    Includes bibliographical references.
    ISBN 0-435-08738-X
    1. Glover, Mary—Biography.   2. Elementary school teachers—Biography. I. Title
LA2317.G57A3   1992
372.11'0092—dc20
[B]   92-27090
                                             CIP

Cover art by Mia Segura
Designed by Jenny Jensen Greenleaf
Printed in the United States of America
93 94 95 96 97   10 9 8 7 6 5 4 3 2 1

For the class of 2000
and for Becky—who held the door open

Blessing Circle

We formed the circle some time ago
Hand in hand we faced its center
   learners one and all
So quickly the circle widened
Letting in our frail and aged comrades
   Wistano who taught us the way of the angels
       Sam   Boot   Anna   Mildred
     lives overflowing with tales both exotic and ordinary

A daily life of literature kept the circle moving
Setting hearts and minds in motion
   shivering in the ocean's depths with Kino and Jiya
    making personal connections to Japanese brothers and sisters
     with rice balls
     paper cranes and a bag of hair
Off we traveled to imaginary worlds
   sneaking sugar in the night with two bad ants
   meeting the Tookies and a talking cat
   learning of bravery and resourcefulness
    from Abel and Dominic
   touched deeply by Aslan's everlasting love

Bravery of another sort seeped into the circle
As we examined the lives of those
Who understood the meaning of sacrifice
   Gandhi   King   and Harriet Tubman

Personal stories and passions kept the circle alive
   How did the Suns do last night?
   And Jenny did you catch another pop fly?
Buddies and body systems
Singing and poetry
Hysterical laughter (get out from under that table please!)
Tears when it's time to say good-bye
A blessing circle sustained by love
Etched forever in the hearts of those
Who kept its life blood flowing

Mary Kenner Glover

Contents

Foreword

Georgia Heard

A teacher works in dreams. We dream of making a better world for children to grow up in. We dream of teaching our students what we have come to believe—sharing our knowledge of the world we live in. We fan the sparks of many children's dreams. Teaching is perhaps the most important job of all because we are the keepers and protectors of so many dreams.

Reading Mary Kenner Glover's book, I am struck by how dreams can turn into reality. When Mary opened the Awakening Seed school in 1977, with her friend Anne Sager, it began with a vision of a place "where people of all walks of life could come together to study and learn from each other." The school's name actually came from a dream "in which seeds were being planted and then were awakening to life." Since that time the seeds have blossomed to an enrollment of one hundred and thirty students. Mary shows us in fascinating detail two years in the life of her first- and second-grade classroom at the Awakening Seed.

She shows us how her day includes a circle of stories and talk: "The circle functioned as the very heart of our classroom life and kept each individual connected to the whole"; how her students build a relationship with elderly people at a local nursing home: "We brought the spirit of youth to the residents and, in turn, they gave us history"; and how writing and poetry are nurtured through what Mary calls a "lively poet's society." Mary shares not only her broad vision but the intimacies and practicalities of everyday classroom life.

The book, subtitled appropriately *A Teacher's Memoir*, is one of the first in a series of accounts by classroom teachers who are observers, questioners, and learners—and therefore, researchers. This is indeed a story of the faces and voices of Mary's first- and second-grade class, but it is also a memoir of Mary's struggles as a teacher returning to the classroom. "My biggest fear . . . was . . . that I had somehow lost touch with that part of myself which, in the past, had been a good teacher of young children. As we sat there in silence that first morning . . . I hoped with all my heart that I would have the patience required to meet the varied needs of this enthusiastic group of students." Every teacher knows this feeling on the first day of school. It is a memoir written for and about teachers.

Especially in this time, when the basic concept of child-centered learning is being challenged—when education magazines carry advertisements for a hot-line for besieged teachers to call if they are in need of support—this book is a refreshing antidote, filled with the voices and learnings of children. In this time, amid the surge of calls to get back to basics, to tests, to rote learning, it's refreshing to read about a classroom where a variety of learning styles is valued. In this time, when teaching kids to care for their community seems a crucial part of our survival, this book is a glass of water amid a great thirst.

This is a beautiful book with a vision of a future. It is an invitation to all of us to dream, to build those dreams, and to share them with others. My thanks to Mary for beginning this important and exciting conversation.

Preface

As I think back on my years of teaching, there are individual students who stand out in my mind—those who will always be remembered as exceptional for one reason or another. They are the inventors, the artists, the scholars, the storytellers. They are the children who, in one way or another, resonate with my own spirit. Often appearing one or two at a time, these children reflect a part of myself that may go unrecognized until I see it expressed through another human being. I have always considered it a great blessing when one of these students appears in my life, for they are rare and precious. They are the ones who always catch me by surprise and teach me things I never dreamed of knowing.

It is even more remarkable when I meet up with an entire group of children with whom I have this personal connection. An opportunity like this happens infrequently, and I am certain that many teachers go through their entire career never having had the chance to know a class in this way. I was fortunate enough to have had a class of students a few years ago where the chemistry between us was right, and we experienced not one but two very magical years together. After it was over I felt that I had no choice but to write about it—for the children, for myself, and for all those teachers who believe in and strive for this kind of experience.

Writing this book was both one of the easiest and most heart-wrenching tasks I have faced as a writer. The experience was richly textured and laden with powerful love and meaning. It was a time that will not be forgotten by any of us who were involved.

I knew I had to write our story for two reasons: to record a historical event in which the children and I participated and to bring a personal closure to the experience. I knew that once written, the story would be finished. As I wrote the final chapter, I felt the pain of having to let go of something very precious and a sense of celebration for having been a part of such a wonderful experience.

Before the story of these two years can be told, it is important to know the context in which it occurred. Founded in 1977, Awakening Seed is a private alternative school located in Tempe, Arizona. My friend Anne Sager and I co-founded the school in my garage with nine very young children, two of whom were my three-year-old and six-month-old daughters. The first inspiration for establishing the school came from our friend Erma Pounds who talked of a school where people of all walks of life could come together to study and learn from each other. I thought it sounded like just the kind of school I'd like my children to attend. She suggested that Anne and I start such a school, and so it began. The school's name actually came from a dream in which seeds were planted and then awoke to life. Awakening Seed seemed like an appropriate name for a school where everyone works together to become more awakened as human beings.

The school has grown from that small group of preschoolers to its current enrollment of 130 students ranging in age from 3 to 10. There are seven classes for preschoolers through the third grade. We have moved several times since the garage days and now have our own building that houses the school's seven classrooms.

When you enter the school's playground through the wrought-iron gate, you'll see children digging in the sand, scooping water from old pots and pans, and chatting underneath the trees. Children of various ages play imaginary games on the tire swings and wooden climbing structures. Around the corner, boys and girls interested in more organized games play on the grass or shoot baskets on the courts. It's not unusual to see younger children and older ones playing together cooperatively.

Inside the building, children's art covers the walls of the hallway. The rooms overflow with learning: insect specimens, maps of the United States and foreign countries, mathematical graphs, examples of children's writing and art, building materials, and large collections of books, to list but a few items. Both children and teachers work together to give their classroom a comfortable lived-in feeling where everybody is welcome.

Awakening Seed's child-centered approach strives to educate the whole child. Children are supported in their cognitive, creative, physical, social, and emotional growth. The school operates under two assumptions: that each person is capable and has strengths to share and that school should be a fun and safe place for everyone. Each teacher has a self-contained classroom, many of which are multiage. All teachers are responsible for planning and implementing the curriculum in all subject areas. Usually several disciplines are integrated into a single content study. During a study of the human body children might make measurements, test out scientific knowledge about the body, record data in logs, write research reports, read all types of information about the body, and express their knowledge through art, poetry, dance, or music. Interests of the teacher and students, as well as local or current events, frequently influence curriculum design. Teachers often collaborate on studies and are eager to share their expertise with each other. Parents and children within the school are also enthusiastic about serving as resources for classroom studies. For example, during the past five years as part of our civil rights study, a parent has come to the school to tell her stories about her participation in the civil rights movement—as the first African-American student to integrate an all-white high school in Virginia.

Awakening Seed's educational philosophy and practice have evolved over the years. Originally, we wanted a program that was fun for the children and at the same time would teach them some values about the world around them. We believed that learning should be interesting and actively engage the minds of our young students. From the very beginning we included activities that would help the children become better citizens of the planet (e.g., picking up litter, visiting a landfill, making up songs about the environment, caring for each other). We also felt that there should be ample opportunities for creative expression. With very little equipment but a range of art materials, we listened to the children's stories, wrote them down, and began to show our young students how speech, literature, and writing fit together. We also read and made frequent trips to the library during those early years. With the help of many people and the addition of new teachers over the years, we have gradually upgraded our program by responding to the needs of our students with the resources available. When we noticed that they needed a larger space and better playground equipment, we enlisted the help of parents who had skills with woodworking. We invested a large portion of our income in classroom libraries so that children would have a good selection of books from which to choose. We were continually asking parents and friends for the raw materials (wood scraps, paper towel tubes, recycled paper, fabric, etc.) for the many projects that arose.

Initially I taught the way I did because it seemed to fit the needs of my own small children and their peers. It made sense to me. As time passed I realized I liked having a sense of autonomy in deciding what should be taught and how. And other teachers kept appearing who felt the same way. All along I've been guided by what I thought was best for my students and what I remember liking and disliking in my own childhood. I have also been surrounded by mentors, friends, and colleagues who have forced me to continually ask Is what I am doing in the best interest of children? I've come to see that my students learn more when their learning is meaningful, active, and project oriented. I've also learned to place more emphasis on children's strengths rather than their weaknesses in everyday work as well as in my assessments of them. Throughout my teaching career, I have tried to stay open to new possibilities and remember that we all learn best when we can share our learning with others.

Besides the school climate, timing influenced this two-year story. Two years before, I had made a decision to leave the classroom for a number of reasons. I wanted to finish my master's degree; I needed a change from the stress of my dual job as director and teacher at the school; and I wanted to pursue a recently acquired interest, dance. Consequently, I maintained my role as the school's director but left the classroom to study dance and finish graduate school. Although I accomplished what I'd set out to, I spent a lot of time questioning which direction I wanted to take with my profession. I wondered whether the classroom was the right place for me—but at the same time, wanted nothing more than to be a teacher again. When an unexpected opportunity arose to teach first grade for the coming school year, it took me only a short time to make my decision. I was going back to the classroom. It didn't take me long to see that teaching was the noblest work I could choose and the only thing I really wanted to do. I also knew it was the only work that would make me happy.

The two weeks I spent in August on the Navajo Reservation helping teachers organize their thinking and practices for holistic teaching took on a more powerful meaning to me, knowing I would soon be putting all of these ideas into action. Working side by side with other teachers, especially my colleagues Linda Sheppard and Maryann Eeds, helped set the stage for my return to the classroom. I was excited about being a teacher again.

My return to the classroom, and particularly to this group of children, taught me many valuable lessons about the strength of the classroom community. I realized how much more we all learn when we work together and help each other grow. The children taught me about the power of a classroom history—a history that involves both the learning that has occurred and the personal relationships that develop between people who live and learn together over time. I was at a point personally and professionally where I was ready to receive these lessons.

I also noticed early on that there is a razor-thin line between work and play and that the two frequently have no separation if the work is interesting and meaningful to the learner. This holds true for teachers as well as children. The hundreds of hours I spent in my classroom preparing materials for school were some of the most pleasurable times I spent during those two years. Knowing what would follow from the children made my work a joyful experience. In the classroom too there was always that blend of work with play in everyday occurrences.

The two years I spent with these children brought on an intense love for my work as a teacher. The rewards were many and always kept things alive and interesting. Although the days were often exhausting, they were also exhilarating. I looked forward to each new day to see what surprises would come along. And they did. This book is about those surprises and the two years of history we created together. It is the story of a teacher and a group of children who shared an unusual enthusiasm for life and learning. It is about people who took the time to care for each other and the things they noticed going on in the world around them. Our story is about the excitement of learning together. And it is about love.

Acknowledgments

In the summers when I was a child, all of the neighborhood kids would gather in our backyard each day for an event we called "the stream." With the garden hose, tiny metal cars, plastic army men, small blocks of wood, and a surplus of sand, rocks, mud, and water, we transformed the ditch behind our house into a world limited only by our imaginations. As we created our village along the stream, our minds seemed to blend into one. It was my first recollection of how it felt to be part of a community.

Thinking back on it, those summers of stream building laid the foundation for much of what this book is about. The time spent with my neighborhood comrades was good practice for learning to create something real out of dreams. The stream days also started me thinking that we all do better when we have other people to help us live our lives. I have come to see, in the process of writing this book, who those people are in my own life. I am grateful for the part each one has played in helping this book come to fruition.

For their love and belief in me, even during the years when I was probably a difficult daughter to love, I have my parents, Jim and Jan Kenner, to thank. They provided me with all the raw materials necessary for the building of streams, as well as a happy childhood.

I could not have taken on my life's work without the guidance and support of my spiritual friend and teacher, Erma Pounds. Years ago she taught me to arise early each morning and begin the day alone in silence. She taught me that through this practice, the mind and its thoughts can be stilled, allowing the voice of intuition, the voice of the heart, to speak. This training set the stage for my approach to teaching as well as our daily classroom practice of silence in circle. In finding a quieter presence within myself, I have been able to pass that on to children in both spoken and unspoken ways. For all of this and more, I am grateful.

I thank my family for helping me develop the inner strength that has allowed me to face each day. My husband Bill reminds me daily that we can't push life for answers or events. Good things, in or out of school, take time and patience. Through his example I have learned to listen more frequently to the voice of my heart, trusting that what is true and right will occur if I am patient. My daughters Sarah and Astraea, in addition to keeping me humble, have given me the opportunity to grow up alongside them, as a mother with daughters but also as friends.

The course of my life, and the person I am, would be much different had it not been for my long-time friend, Anne Metzger Horey. From the moment we met in the throes of youth, I have known that regardless of whatever happened, I would always have a friend. Knowing this has given me the courage to take risks and try the untried even when I knew the stakes were high.

There are many people to thank in my professional life. My interest in the telling of stories, particularly school stories, has been encouraged by two of my colleagues, Maryann Eeds, a professor in children's literature at Arizona State University, and Linda Sheppard, a local kindergarten teacher. It was during the days we spent together as consultants on the Navajo Reservation that the beginnings of this story surfaced, particularly on our frequent after-hours road trips to Canyon de Chelly, Mexican Hat, Utah, and other locations in the Monument Valley area. Maryann valued the school stories Linda and I told about our classrooms and encouraged us to continue telling them.

The person who has been most influential in helping me develop my teaching practice is Ralph Peterson, a professor at Arizona State University. Both friend and mentor, Ralph is a continuing source of inspiration and encouragement in my life. He has always valued my stories and helped me to recognize their preciousness. I am thankful for his presence in my life.

I also want to thank two other university professors, Elaine Surbeck and Michael Kelley, who spent a considerable amount of time conducting research in my room. Elaine and Michael offered insights and asked questions that helped lead my work into new and exciting directions. They also shared my appreciation for the humorous aspect of my teaching life and encouraged me to keep thinking and writing.

On a daily basis I have been supported by my fellow staff members at Awakening Seed. Yvonne Mersereau, in particular, has not only helped me make major theoretical leaps but has also assisted me in surviving the day-to-day demands of teaching. She has taught me to laugh at situations I have perhaps taken too seriously and follow up on those which need more attention. During the first grade year I had the good fortune of working alongside Becky Lewis, who served as my classroom assistant. Becky and I had on-going conversations, both spoken and written (in a dialogue journal) about everything we noticed happening in our room. Becky helped me think through everything I did and articulate what I thought about life in our classroom. Debra Kalior, a parent and graduate student, also spent time in our room each week. Her questions inspired me to read more in order to broaden my theoretical base. Along with Becky and Debra, our class was fortunate to have had two exceptional student teachers. Cecelia Espinoza, a native of Ecuador, enriched all of our lives in first grade through her unique insights as a foreign citizen. Desireé Pierone, my student teacher during the second grade year, carried with her, among many wonderful qualities, a love for song. Through her passion for music Desireé taught us that each person's voice counts—strong or weak, loud or soft—and the music isn't complete without the voice of every person. Kathy and Michael Shores, Kerri Tornow, Sandi Autrey, Terry Heyl, and Carol Bishton have also shown their support and helped make it a pleasure to come to work each day. To these staff members and all of the other people at Awakening Seed I'm unable to name individually, I am deeply indebted.

Another collection of people, indirectly involved in my everyday classroom life, are the individuals I have met through local organizations, university courses, or seminars. Karen Smith, then a classroom teacher, showed me a way to organize my holistic teaching practice years ago and has continued to promote my work as a teacher. Pam Matt at the ASU Dance Department gave me two wonderful years of dance and conversation that renewed my spirit and allowed me to return to the classroom. Pam Clark, Diana Doyle, Carol Edelsky, Joan Moyer, Virginia Opincar, and Caryl Steere, among others, have also guided me at various stages of my career.

I am grateful to Carol Christine and the staff at the Center for Establishing Dialogue in Teaching and Learning (CED) for their efforts to support teachers. My work as a teacher and writer has been shaped by the well-known individuals CED has brought to Phoenix for seminars and keynote addresses. The opportunity to personally meet and study with Donald Murray, Mary Ellen Giacobbe, Pat Carini, Georgia Heard, and Vivian Paley has been a gift.

I'd also like to thank the two people who have directly helped me with this book. First, I want to express my gratitude to Georgia Heard for writing the foreword and for becoming my friend when she did. Meeting Georgia was a turning point in my life as a writer, and it was after we first met that I was able to face revising the initial manuscript. Finally, I offer my deepest thanks to Dawne Boyer, my editor at Heinemann. Dawne was able to see the potential in that first manuscript, and she took the time to make suggestions that not only made the book better but allowed me to grow as a writer. Her gentle touch and advice to follow my own instincts as a writer always made me feel respected and honored—as a writer and as a person.

Our Way of Beginning

❧ On one of the first days of first grade, I passed out the new September journals. After writing and drawing for 10 or 15 minutes, six-year-old Emily approached me. A gentle and lovable child, I'd known Emily since she was three years old and had looked forward to being her teacher one day. In her hand she held her journal and offered it with a smile. She was eager to share her first entry of the year. (See Figure 1–1.) In that brief moment I realized that my decision to return to the classroom after two years of graduate school was indeed the correct one. When I saw what Emily had written, I never again questioned whether I'd made the right decision.

Actually I hadn't intended to teach that year. I'd been away from the daily business of classroom life for two years and had almost convinced myself that my classroom teaching days were over. Almost. But that was not to be the case. Last minute changes landed me back in the thick of it all. When the second-grade teacher left, it allowed the same children and me to remain together for second grade. It was a two year odyssey that profoundly altered the course of my teaching life.

My biggest fear in returning to the classroom was that I had perhaps lost my edge, that I had somehow lost touch with a part of myself that, in the past, had been a good teacher of young children. As we sat there in silence that first morning (a ritual we were to repeat every morning), I hoped with all my heart that I would have the patience required to meet the varied needs of this enthusiastic group of students. Quite honestly, I wondered if I were doing the right thing by returning to the classroom. I was more than a little bit nervous I might not have what I knew it would take to teach these children. As I looked at each one of those eager faces, I knew I had to try.

The foundation for beginning those early days, and all the days that followed, was our meeting circle. Each morning we started by sitting together on the floor in a circle. (Afternoons were begun in a similar fashion with a shortened version of the morning circle.) In the circle each face could be seen and each person held an equal place within the group. It was here that we set up routines and worked out

9/2/88 M I

Mary, it is fun having you for a teacher. Are you proud to be a teacher?

Mary it is fun having you for a techr An you Prawd to Be a techr?

FIGURE 1–1 *Emily's first journal entry*

a plan for keeping our room running smoothly. Among the topics covered were

- assigning clean-up jobs (e.g., sweeping floors, wiping off tables, vacuuming the floors) and explaining how to carry them out
- taking attendance
- explaining fire drill procedures
- establishing rules of conduct (*Work hard. Do your best. Be kind.*)
- homework procedures and policies
- finding solutions to playground safety issues
- classroom schedules and plans
- how to handle relationships within the classroom

In those first few days of school, our meeting circle helped us to come together as a learning community with concentrated energy. We were able to get things established smoothly from the beginning. As time passed, our circle became a forum in which we made our plans for special events, such as our Japanese festival, and later evaluated their successes and shortcomings. It was where we talked about the world and our responsibilities as world citizens. The circle functioned as the very heart of our classroom life and kept each individual connected to the whole. It was where we laughed and cried as a group of people who cared deeply about each other. Our daily opening circle had four parts: silence, story, talk, and song.

Silence

The 9:00 bell has just rung and 19 agitated bodies stream into the room. Children are laughing and fooling around. Coats are tossed into cubbies and drinks are slurped at the drinking fountain in the hallway. Brian has to use the restroom, and Mia handles taking attendance. Jessica checks the list and discovers that it is her day to ring the bell. After considerable squirming and moving around, along with a reminder for Ben to please come out from under the table, each person takes his or her place in the circle, and we prepare for silence and the beginning of a new day. I remind the children to place themselves into a comfortable position so they won't be touching another person's body. I tell them to close their eyes and suggest they clear their minds of any thoughts, just allow their minds to be still in preparation for the day. I ask them to be aware of their breathing, to slow it down, and to take deep breaths. When everyone is prepared, Jessica rings the bell to begin the silence. Some bodies remain still with quiet, concentrated breathing. Despite their best efforts, others can't seem to keep their hands from moving or their eyes closed. They notice latecomers and any distracting noises. After a minute or two, when she feels the group is ready, Jessica again rings the bell to bring the silence to a close. We are ready to attend to the school day's business.

The essence the circle was in those few minutes of silence we shared each day. The whole day rested on the silence. Some days I would suggest they hold a specific thought in mind, such as healing for a sick friend or a special goal for the day. On Earth Day, for example, we thought of healing the earth, simultaneously visualizing a healthy, harmonious planet. The silence was a time for remembering we are individually part of a greater whole. It gave us time each day to just *be* together. It allowed us to focus and prepare ourselves for the coming hours we would share together.

Story

Our daily practice of silence is completed. Elizabeth has finished taking attendance. She counts the number of students present and adds this information to the bottom of the sheet in the event that we have a fire drill and have to count heads. She returns the clipboard to its proper place and joins her peers for the next phase of the group meeting.

I ask if anyone has a story to tell. Jenny sheepishly raises her hand. I am surprised by this act of boldness by a child who usually sits on the outer fringes of the circle, taking it all in but seldom offering a word. Jenny—bright, freckle-faced, compact, and athletic—shines as she quickly tells her T-ball story: "Last night I caught a pop fly. Our team got them out and we won the game." We are all impressed by Jenny's athletic accomplishment and even more proud of her for finding the courage to share the story with our class. Instantly she is held in high regard by everyone in the class. She is clearly the celebrity of the day. Her story gives us a glimpse into her world and allows her to feel safer about sharing herself with the rest of the community.

The stories which came to our circle were rich and varied. Some were very funny—such as Ben's. The class laughed hysterically as he told us how he had tried to photograph a horse in Vancouver but only managed to get the horse's read end in the picture. Other stories, like the one Katie told us about her great-grandmother dying, made us cry. There were essentially two types of stories that occurred: our own stories and the stories of others outside our community; specifically through literature. As we told and listened to stories, we came to understand the power of story for understanding each other and the world in which we live.

Some days I would have to ask if anyone had a story to tell. A few children asked ahead of time. Jessica asked me one day, "Can I do my sharing before April 14th [her designated sharing day]? It'll be dead by then!" After further prodding, she informed me that her sharing was a large leaf. Her sharing and her story could not wait.

Frequently, the children would bring artifacts to accompany their stories. One of my favorites was Jacob's collection of plastic bags of different colors of sand, each with its own story. He told of each place he and his dad had stopped in Utah and northern Arizona to collect the bags full of colorful silica. And there was the morning when Tara paraded into the room with her father's boa constrictor skin. She announced to the entire class, "I think it would be a good idea to do a math activity with it. We should measure it after we look at it and touch it." Noah's story about the birds flying into his house in Louisiana unleashed all kinds of bird stories. And Caitlin fascinated everyone with her photographs and description of the inside-out building she saw in France on her trip with her father that summer.

Our stories, both the children's and my own, were what helped to build a rich history. They helped us to know each other in a way that was both private and public at the same time. These stories gave us insight into the personal life of each individual and became a collective source of information about each other from which we all worked. When the Phoenix Suns basketball team won a big game over the Lakers, everyone in the class knew how thrilled Charlie would be. The day Jacob's brother came for a visit from California we didn't need to ask why Jacob had such a huge grin on his face. We felt his joy because we knew his stories: he was part of our community, and he was a part of all of us. As we grew together, individually and as a community, our history was created from these stories. We daily cultivated and enriched this history as we added new stories to the collection.

The other stories that gave life to our circle were those written by authors outside our classroom. Our own stories were what each of us brought to the circle, much like a clearing in the forest. They were our personal offerings to the rest of the group. The stories of others, those not physically present in our classroom, became the road that took us away from the clearing, along which we traveled together. They all helped our minds and hearts to grow. Further on, an entire chapter is devoted to examining the role that literature played in our classroom and the spirit it brought to our learning community.

Talk

Sweaty bodies burst through the doorway after their noon-hour recess. It is April in Arizona, and the weather is getting hot. Tempers are even hotter and feelings have been hurt. One child, red faced and tearful, storms through the door and heads for the pillow corner. Clearly there is trouble. Before going on to the afternoon schedule, we talk it out; each child having his or her say concerning the matter.

I ask a couple of the girls to tell me their version of what happened. It appears that someone has been telling secrets again. Arguing briefly erupts. The child blamed for telling secrets defends herself in tears. The two who have told on her also start crying, but eventually everyone is able to air their feelings. I remind the class that school should always be a safe place for everyone, physically and emotionally. I also remind them that if we are to live in a peaceful world, it has to begin where we are at school. After a few more tears, the girls involved in the incident finally hug each other and offer apologies. We are now ready to move ahead.

Talking, in this case, has helped us settle our differences and has renewed our respect for each other. Talk allowed us to negotiate our problems and show we cared. It enabled us to heal the wounds that sometimes injured our circle and return it to a whole and healthy condition.

Talk and story are highly interconnected. Stories could not occur without talk. But talk was sometimes independent of story within our circle. We frequently had business to take care of such as planning projects for the day; discussing the weather, world topics, or how to handle the mechanics of writing (e.g., spelling, punctuation); critiquing our own writing or that of others; or organizing information for a class study. In our circle, we talked about everything that was exciting and interesting to our class. We talked to make meaning of the world around us. Gordon Wells (1986) says

> Conversation is rarely an end in itself, particularly where young children are concerned. They talk in order to achieve other ends: to share their interest in the world around them, to obtain the things they want, to get others to help them, to participate in the activities of the grown-up world, to learn how to do things or why things are as they are, or just to remain in contact. . . . In the process, a great deal of information is called forth, either as a necessary adjunct to the performance of activities or because it is judged to be of interest in itself. (p. 53)

Talk kept our classroom alive. It was the pulse of our classroom life. Through talk (or the absence of it) I was able to know the children who were passionately committed to their work and those still searching for a topic that would kindle the fire of enthusiasm in their hearts and minds. Through talk, I learned that we had several gerbil lovers in our class and some who thought the little rodents were disgusting. I discovered that Denise loved to play chess, and Brian was in Cub Scouts with Noah. Talk gave me insights into the thinking and interests of my students.

Talk was the instrument by which we measured how far we'd come and the determiner of where we needed to venture next. When Adrin said, "Drafts of writing are like baby talk," she meant that as we practice and get better at writing we mature. We outgrow it and move on to other stages. The same idea applied to talk in our classroom. As we worked at it, talking to each other, we got better at it. It enabled us to process much of what arose in our lives, both in and out of school. Talk allowed us to work and grow together as learners; and it gave us a means by which to create our own class history.

Song

We complete our morning business. A few stories are exchanged, but nobody is ready to move on to writing yet. The energy in our circle is marginally rowdy. One of the children asks, "Can we sing today? How about 'Mr. Frog'? We promise we won't get too wild." I remind them that we can't do "Mr. Frog " because it will disturb the class next door, but we could sing something else. Without being asked, Jessica gets out my guitar, and we agree on a quieter song. The singing is particularly good today, so we continue with a few more songs. After 15 minutes everyone is satisfied, and we're ready to get serious about writing.

Singing helped to bond us together as we approached each new day of learning and living in our classroom. The songs we shared created a sense of celebration in our hearts for the whole range of the human experience. We sang silly songs that made us loosen up and laugh. We sang songs with histories. We sang songs about war and the struggle for human rights. Some songs we shared were those early childhood melodies passed down from generation to generation, songs sung for old time's sake. When we sang "Go Tell Aunt Rhody" for our friends at the nursing home, one of the residents, Boot Hill, cried because it reminded him of his childhood days. Boot told us that his aunt who raised him had sung that song to him when he was a little boy. When he told us this story, it added new meaning to the song the next time we sang it in class. His story reminded us how songs can connect people over time and distance. It made us want to sing even more.

Singing helped us feel like we were a family. It connected us. When everything else failed to pull us together as a group, singing brought us back together. Our songs reminded us that we each have a responsibility to use our voice—for singing and to make the world a better place. One of our school songs, "Celebrate Life on Planet Earth," expresses this perspective:

> Now is the time we all have to give
> Open our hearts so the Earth can live
> To all living creatures under the sun
> We give our lives so we can be One
>
> Celebrate life on planet Earth
> This is the home of our human birth
> Celebrate love on planet Earth
> Live your life for all it's worth

As we sat in our circle at the beginning of each day—first in silence, then with talk, stories, and song—we prepared ourselves for the important work that lay ahead of us. We gathered as a group of kindred spirits, eager to know more about the unfolding world around us. With the ritual of our opening circle completed, we were primed for the business at hand: we were ready for another day of school. We were ready to learn.

Common Threads

2

ଽ☚ No two days were ever alike. Although we always began each day with our group meeting, what followed was much like an artist's monoprint—each one was unique and filled with surprises. There was, of course, a framework in which spontaneous and exciting events happened. Our daily schedule looked something like this:

9:00–9:30	morning circle
9:30–10:45	writing/author sharing
10:45–11:05	recess
11:05–12:00	math
12:00–1:00	lunch/recess
1:00–2:15	read aloud/silent reading/lit study
2:15–3:00	content studies/art/special classes

Some days we followed our plan closely; other days we hardly touched on the first agenda item. Even though each day was exceptional in its own way, there were common threads that tied our days together. Those threads were of two types: predictable and spontaneous.

The planned daily events in which we participated (writing, mathematics, reading and literature study, art, and content studies) and the weekly activities such as creative movement, visits to the nursing home, buddy reading (see Chapter 3), physical education (P.E.), and music class were predictable. Spontaneity usually appeared within the course of a planned activity. Some spontaneous events were so powerful they stood on their own, but most of them happened this way:

A Typical Day

We finish our morning circle. Writing workshop is about to begin. A few days ago I had worked with Jessica on putting spaces between words when she writes. At the time it didn't appear that she grasped the concept, but I assumed she would catch on sooner or later. This morning before school I noticed, as I was glancing through the journals, that she had gone back over her writing and erased what she'd written. She had rewritten her message with spaces between the words. I made the decision to use Jessica's discovery as the mini-lesson for the day since I knew there were others in the class who also struggled with the spacing concept.

During the writing workshop, I ask Jessica to explain to the class what she has learned. She says, "You can read it better with the spaces." We all applaud Jessica for her growth as a writer and go on with the lesson. After a brief demonstration on the chalkboard about the benefits of putting spaces between words, we move on to writing.

Jessie and Maureen pass out writing folders, pencils are sharpened, markers are pulled from the shelf and set out on the tables. The room is filled with the noise of writers settling into their work. We try for 10 minutes of silent sustained writing, but it's a struggle. Ideas are flying around the room and several writers find it impossible to be quiet. I walk around with my clipboard and check in with each child. Everyone is beginning to settle into work. Noah is starting a new piece after completing his first one. Several other children have done the same. Ben brings me a page he has written about his aunt's dog bumping into a tree in Wisconsin. He wrote "AWTH" coming out of the dog's mouth, and underneath it he has written an upside-down exclamation point. He comments, "I made a statement there."

I notice J. J. meticulously digging through a bag of gerbil food trying to find out exactly what is contained in it. He hasn't written anything, but he is gathering information about what gerbils eat. He is completely absorbed in his research. Tara is requesting her usual daily conference with me, and I tell her to set up a conference sign-up list on the board. I ask her to wait until I've checked in with everyone else.

Caitlin is writing about her dog that ran away when she lived in Chinle, in northern Arizona. She says, "I'm done." As she starts to put her folder away, I ask her what she will do next. Caitlin looks at her draft and says, "Oh, I have to read it over." She reads her piece and exclaims, "It's not done!" She revises a few words, then reads her ending. "That's not right—it says 'THE AND,' not 'THE END'!" We look at each other with a smile. I move on to Adrin. I modeled a conference with her for the whole class the day before and wonder what she has done with her draft. She is still thinking. I move on to Tara, who is waiting patiently for her conference.

Tara and I talk about the possibility of publishing her "Grampy" piece. She is, of course, enthusiastic about publication. We talk briefly about editing, and I ask her to check her draft for misspelled words and circle a few she notices. She glances at her paper and says, "Well,

I can see one right here. This says 'ham', not 'him'." I leave her to her work, curious to see what she does with her newly acquired editing skill.

I glance at the clock and notice we have run out of time to have author sharing today. I make a quick decision to skip it and ring the bell to notify everyone that it is time for recess. After a whirlwind process of stuffing papers into folders, putting caps on markers and returning them to the shelf, shoving chairs under the tables, and grabbing snacks, we depart to the playground to unwind.

When recess is over, we return to the classroom. We move right into mathematics. It's early in the year, and children are freely exploring the math materials. They take the materials they are interested in and go to work. Caitlin and J. J., two of my regular daydreamers, are deeply engrossed in sorting out the new collection of beads I have just added to the junk box tub. They make patterns as they carry on an intense conversation. I wish I had my camera. Over at the weighing station, Jessica and Emily have created an entire world of dinosaurs, pattern blocks, and small objects. They incorporate their play with the scales, weighing various small items as their fantasy grows. I suggest that they might want to record this activity in their math notebooks. They consider my idea as I move on to the rice station where Maureen and Denise have turned the large container of rice into a treasure hunt by adding glass beads to the quantity of rice. They take turns hiding the beads, then make each other find them, counting as they go. I hear other counting in the room. I notice Jacob has spearheaded a project connecting all the Unifix cubes in our room. The colorful train contains 460 cubes as it leaves our room and overflows into the hallway. Another glance at the clock tells me it's already past lunch time. I ask Katie to ring the bell and inform everyone that it's time to clean up. A loud and rather chaotic clean-up period follows, but eventually all math materials are put away and the major social event of the day occurs: lunch.

Lunch boxes bang about on the tables as grimy hands are reluctantly washed and territories established. The boys, being only six, stick together at one table. Jenny is the only girl who ever dares enter their space. I remind them about appropriate table manners if they would like to remain seated together for the entire lunch period. Thermos caps are removed, straws are unwrapped, sandwiches are stuffed rapidly into talking mouths, and conversation abounds.

Ben and his buddies are beginning to fool around. I say, "Ben, if you would like to remain at the table with your friends, you need to use appropriate manners." With a charming smile on his face he says, "Yes, Mary." Within minutes he has squished his raisins on the floor and squeezed juice out the straw of his juice box all over Jacob's lunch. Jacob is clearly unhappy, and nobody is eating their lunch at Ben's table. I give Ben one of those looks that clearly tells him I am not pleased with his behavior. I simply say "Ben" and motion where I would like him to move. He finishes his lunch at another table without further incident. Children complete the task of eating and return empty lunch boxes to their cubbies. The clean-up crew goes to work.

J. J. has been assigned table duty this week. He looks at the collection of wrappers and crumbs of food on the table and exclaims, "This is disgusting! Mary, we need to talk to the kids about cleaning up their messes better!" I agree and ask him to mention it during the afternoon circle. He reluctantly scoops the mess into the trash can, completes his job, and goes outside with the rest of his classmates for lunch recess.

Our afternoon is no less busy than the morning. After silence and a brief discussion about the messy lunch tables, we prepare for our read-aloud time. Today I have chosen *Yonder* by Tony Johnston. I read as some children lie down to listen and others sit close by my feet. When I have finished the book I ask all of them to sit up in a circle, and we begin our dialogue. They respond favorably to *Yonder*. I am pleased because it is a serious book and they have a lot to say about it. It is encouraging to know that they appreciate reflective stories as well as those that make them laugh.

Jennifer comments, "The story starts all over. The generations go on and on. The family isn't the same people, but it's still a family." J. J. adds, "The story recycles. It starts all over with new people." Tara is observant in noting that the family in the story plants trees on important days, when a new baby is born or when someone dies. Ben says, "They planted trees to remember people on sad or exciting days." As our discussion comes to a close, I remind myself to read the book again on another day to see what additional ideas they bring to it.

Eager readers are anxious to pursue their own books, so we break up the large group to begin our half hour of silent (theoretically) independent reading. Children pull out their reading logs in which they record the daily titles they read, collect the books they'll need, and settle in to a comfortable spot in the room. Brian grabs everything he needs and heads for the loft. Jessie, Mia, Tara, Jessica, and Caitlin assemble as a group together on the floor to read *Come*

Away from the Water, Shirley. They make a decision to take turns reading the text. I am pleasantly surprised by how well Mia is reading. When it is Tara's turn, she passes. Caitlin gives it a try. She really works at it and relies heavily on the illustrations. Caitlin reads "kids" for "children" and "rocks" for "stones." Without being too instructive, I comment that actually the words are "children" and "stones." Jessica, who has mostly been observing this impromptu reading group chimes in, "Does it really matter? Why do you have to say 'children' instead of 'kids'? What's the difference?" I explain to her that the meaning doesn't really change if you read one or the other in this case, but the letters on the page are there to remind you to say certain words. I tell her that there will be times with other books where it's important to read the exact word. We talk about this a bit more, and I move on to other readers. When it is time for silent reading to be over, I ask everyone to put their books away. Brian, who has been deeply engrossed in his book in the loft, asks, "Hey! When are we going to do silent reading?" I make a mental note of this reader who has truly been lost in his text!

When books are put away and titles are recorded in logs, we have just enough time left in the afternoon to work on our content study of the aging process. We pick up our previous day's discussion about the skin and make a quick chart list of how it changes. It is decided that your skin gets thinner, darker, and drier as you age. Using the magnifying glasses we have borrowed from the third graders, the children examine each other's skin up close. Among the most noticeable items are freckles, wrinkles, gray hairs (on my head, of course), mosquito bites, and cuts. Tara exclaims that she noticed some "unreal" skin on Jennifer. When asked to elaborate she explains that she saw some skin where there were no freckles, and it seemed unreal because most other places did have freckles. Other comments are shared and the day ends with an assignment to go home and interview parents about their attitudes on aging, including how it feels to have their skin change. When homework folders are distributed and lunch boxes are collected along with assorted papers and other paraphernalia, the children depart for their lives beyond the classroom. I sit down, take a few deep breaths, and start to think about tomorrow.

When You Least Expect It

Our everyday life was, of course, constantly altered by the planned special events or classes that occurred. Music and P.E. took the children away from the classroom and allowed them the opportunity to extend themselves in new directions without me. We veered from our daily routine to dance, to read with our three-year-old buddies, and to visit our friends at the nursing home. But we never became so tightly attached to our schedule that there was no room for the spontaneous threads that wove in and out of our lives unexpectedly. We always tried to make time to walk to a nearby park on a sunny spring day or set aside our work to watch the cement trucks add their contributions to the construction going on next door. I found myself frequently revising the daily schedule according to special events, the time of year, or particular needs of the children. When we studied Japan (Glover, 1990), we dropped everything for two weeks so we could finish up our projects in time for the festival we had planned. In December our room looked like Santa's workshop as we illustrated poetry and memoirs, sewed self-portraits of burlap and yarn, and rehearsed for our upcoming winter solstice performance for the parents.

We also made time for special people connected to our class who had talents and time to share. Terry, the school maintenance director, often came into our classroom to assist with projects that required skilled hands and the proper tools. When we came up with the glorious plan to make a life-sized papier-mâché skeleton, he meticulously helped us assemble it with wire, paper fasteners, and an assortment of other gadgets. The children took turns with Terry adding their set of bones to the whole structure. We spent a delightful afternoon with our friend Pam who brought in her human skeleton when we studied bones in first grade. It was a treat to be able to touch a real skeleton and have so many of our questions answered by an expert.

Time was also allowed for talented parents who wanted to come in to make special contributions to our class. When we did our Japanese study, Jessica's mom not only brought in laundry baskets full of books about Japan, but she arranged for a tea ceremony and origami instruction with two Japanese college students. We spent a morning with them, tasting the green ceremonial tea and learning to fold paper miraculously into cranes. When it came time for our feast, she organized our massive food production line in preparation for the multitude of guests we had invited. On another morning Brian's mom took time off from her busy teaching schedule to give us an art lesson on texturing. And Mia's mom brought a friend to our class one day with masks, artifacts, and history about the Mexican celebration of the Day of the Dead. They took our pictures with the masks on, served us a drink made especially for the occasion, and let us touch all their skeleton miniatures. These special events enriched our already lively days and added a texture to the experience that would have otherwise been missing. They inspired us to look beyond life at school with our eyes opened more widely to the world.

Other unexpected segments of our days were often taken up with the small duties necessary for maintaining our school facility. We knew that Terry and Bill, the two people responsible for this job, depended on our assistance to keep everything running smoothly. They brought the realities of school management into our lives and encouraged us to be active participants in the process. Bill requested written notification if anything around the school needed repair or replacement. During his tenure as business and facility manager, he received requests for a broad range of items, including gerbil food, soap in the girls' bathroom, and a swimming pool complete with a diving board. The repair reminders, which Bill frequently found taped to his office door, involved everything from cleaning the sand out of the outside drinking fountain to fixing the drips in the bathrooms. Ben provided one of the more entertaining requests the day he came running down the hall from the bathroom exclaiming, "Mary, there's a problem with that thing on the wall in the boys' bathroom!" I asked him to write it down and give the note to Bill so he could attend to it. Ben's note is shown in Figure 2–1.

Both Bill and Terry demonstrated through their actions the kind of care needed to physically keep a school community operating. They helped us learn to pay attention to even the smallest of details and take time from our day to be actively responsible for our school's well-being. They reminded us that the time we took to care for our environment was equally important to the time spent learning to read and write. In fact, they showed us ways we could use our abilities as readers and writers to be helpful around the school. When Elizabeth and Maureen accidentally spilled paint on the sign by the sink in the three-year-old classroom, they had no hesitation in replacing it. (See Figure 2–2.) Their acquired skills as writers helped them to act quickly to remedy the situation.

The flexibility of our schedule, and our willingness to remain wide open to the unexpected, kept our days alive and filled with possibility. Our class, in many ways, was like any other group of learners. We worked daily to care for each other, to establish and maintain a classroom environment that was conducive to safety and well-being. We were involved in learning that was exciting and at the same time informative. Our class was a committed group of readers and writers,

FIGURE 2–1 *Ben's note to Bill*

scientists, and mathematicians who wanted to know about the world. We established relationships with others outside our immediate classroom who were important to us. We cared—about learning, each other, the natural world around us, and the people in it.

But there was an additional quality about these children that set them apart from any other group I have taught. It may have been the history established by years of growing up in the same school together, and especially the opportunity to stay together as a class with the same teacher for two years. Or it might have been the workings of

FIGURE 2–2   *Elizabeth and Maureen's note about the soap sign*

chance that so many individuals with such a zest for life were placed together for a short while.

Regardless of what brought us together, it was clear what made us different. It was the level of intensity with which we approached the predictable work of daily life and learning. It was the incredible ability to laugh and be playful with each other, and at the same time offer sensitivity and comfort when needed. It was our capacity for recognizing the value of spontaneity and being able to go with the unexpected when it arose. It was our willingness to entertain the outrageous and always push the edges of possibility. What set us apart as a gathering of kindred spirits was our ability to love—our work, those around us, and each other. What follows is the result of that love.

3 Significant Others

🎶 Our days together were nothing less than exuberant. There was a continual supply of exciting experiences leaping back and forth between our classroom and the rest of the world. We kept our eyes wide open to possibilities for learning and change. This occurred through the things we wrote about, the books we read, and the studies we pursued. It also happened as a result of the other people we let into our lives.

In the previous chapter I mentioned the special guests, parents, and significant others who joined us from time to time, enriching our classroom life. Two other groups of people, at opposite ends of the age spectrum, also joined us on a more regular basis. They were our friends at a nearby nursing home and our reading buddies from the three-year-old class. Both contributed to our lives in ways we would not have experienced otherwise. They helped us see where we fit in the cycle of life. They enabled us to know ways in which we could develop further as loving, caring human beings.

New Life with Old Friends

Our visits to the nursing home didn't just happen spontaneously. They evolved out of years of careful planning by teachers, doctors, and other individuals interested in geriatrics and education. Our class was invited to be one of the pilot groups for a newly established intergenerational program called Community. The goal of the Community program was to enrich the lives of the residents and children through intergenerational friendships. Our plan was to visit a nursing home each week and incorporate that experience into the curriculum.

To prepare the children for the visits we began reading books a month beforehand that dealt with issues of aging. One of the first stories I read the children was *Wilfrid Gordon McDonald Partridge*. Mem Fox's story is about a young boy who lived next to a nursing home. In the story the boy helps an old woman remember special moments in her life and in the process their friendship is deepened. That story and others such as *Tales of a Gambling Grandma*, *Nana Upstairs and Nana Downstairs*, and *Grandmama's Joy*, set the stage for two years with elder friends. In addition to our reading, we explored numerous issues related to the aging process and the life cycle (see Chapter 4). We had a visitor from Oregon, who had worked with children in nursing homes before. She taught us how to maneuver wheelchairs, handle "grabbers" who loved children so much they were reluctant to let go, and informed us of the unique smells, sounds, and other experiences we might encounter at the nursing home. We were well prepared when the day of the first visit arrived. As time passed relationships were established, and the children gained confidence entering into this new situation. This early December visit was typical:

The energetic collection of six- and seven-year-olds files out the classroom door, carrying containers of glue, wax paper, yarn, scissors, and an assortment of beans and seeds for making holiday ornaments. I ask Katie and Jessica to bring my guitar because I know I can trust them to carry it to the bus without dropping it. Everyone hustles down the hallway, chattering excitedly in anticipation of the day's visit. In a slightly congested manner, we board the bus, which has just arrived to pick us up from Westchester Care Center.

The bus ride is noisy and happy. When we reach the nursing home, a steady stream of excited bodies flows from the bus. We are happy to see Mildred and Olive waiting for us, just as eagerly, at the shaded entrance. Hugs are given out, and we enter the nursing home together. We set up the materials as children disappear into the hallways to bring their favorite resident to the meeting room, and another successful visit is underway.

On this particular day the planned project is to make ornaments by gluing seeds and beans on wax paper in various shapes. Yarn is attached to hang the ornament when it is dry. The children are eager to get started, so they gather their necessary materials, find willing residents, and wheel them to the closest table. I notice that a few children seem to be missing. I discover them in an adjacent room with several residents and the Mary Kay lady who has come for the morning to give facials. Noah, Jacob, and Adrin, each with a cotton ball in hand, are generously applying facial cream to a resident's wrinkled face. Noah looks like an artist putting the finishing touches on a masterpiece. His tongue protrudes from his mouth as he works on the ancient face with complete concentration. The residents glow with all this personal attention.

Back in the main room, Sam has gathered a large following around his wheelchair. Decked out in a brightly colored stocking cap, he shares his Jewish heritage with the children, explaining the story of Hanukkah. He is quite the storyteller! In a while he takes this same group to his room to give them chocolate candy and dreydels. (The event was later recorded by Adrin in her journal when she wrote, "Sam gave some of the kids candy. Sam's a honaka.")

The ornament making is going well. Some of the children are quite skillful at getting the residents involved in making ornaments. Others make the ornaments while the residents watch, at the residents' request. Hazel seems a bit disgruntled because she wants to make her own. Jennifer has chosen to work with Alta who can be difficult at times. Today Jennifer works with amazing patience as she gently reminds Alta not to eat the seeds or pull the yarn off the completed but not yet dry ornaments. Boot, a popular resident with the boys, seems drowsy today. Perhaps he is tired from his recent job of delivering the residents' mail to them. Mildred, another favorite, has a flock of girls around her. Her friendliness and accessibility for conversation make her very popular. Even Jenny, who is painfully shy, loves to snuggle up and talk to Mildred. The morning is charged with that precious delight that friends, young and old, feel when they know they are loved.

This visit and all those that followed during the next two years became a life experience that had a profound impact on all of us. We found our circle of friends widening as we stepped into the lives of these people. Each week we would greet them with art projects, books, games, and songs. In all of us there was a wellspring of compassion emerging from places deep within us. Connections made with residents often went beyond words. I can still remember six-year-old Jennifer approaching me during our first visit. With tears sparkling in her eyes and slightly trembling, she said, "Mary, I picked the one I want." She had chosen Alta, a pretty woman with white hair and a pink dress. Later, on two separate occasions, she wrote about Alta in her journal:

> I found a person that looked like my aunt. She can't talk very good but she feels special. I tell her jokes. I love her. I saw her again when I came to the nursing home. I did see her but I saw her again. I kissed her. She said she couldn't kiss back and I waited awhile and she kissed me. I was excited.

After just two visits Alta began saying, "I love you" to Jennifer and

Jessie, who made it their responsibility to take care of her. The nursing home staff reported that Alta hadn't spoken in months prior to our visits.

Other friendships formed between children and residents. Editha, who couldn't remember how old she was or how many children she had, always greeted us with a smile of recognition. She was delighted on the day when the Mary Kay lady arrived at the nursing home for the facials, and six-year-old Adrin, cotton swab in hand, applied the facial creme gently and lovingly to her delicate, wrinkly skin. A year later when Tara approached her for an interview for the school newspaper, Editha responded with the same joyful enthusiasm, even though her health had deteriorated, and she was completely bedridden. It seemed more like a dance between the two, watching Tara ask her questions and Editha thoughtfully responding. Even though Editha's responses were confused and disjointed, Tara listened to every word and carefully wrote them on her paper. In the end they both felt a sense of dignity, having honored each other in the deepest sense.

We brought the spirit of youth to the residents and, in turn, they gave us history. The past came alive through their amazing stories. Sam always drew a large gathering with his adventures of early days in Russia when the Czar was still in power. On one occasion he held Noah, Charlie, and Jacob spellbound for 45 minutes as he told them the tale of his hand-carved wooden cane with the snake on it. He said it had been carved by an Indian friend. One-hundred-year-old Anna was no less charming with her accounts of life in Germany and later when she served as a cook for the Reagan family in California. One of the few residents not in a wheelchair, Anna inspired us all with her fresh, optimistic outlook on life. When asked how she was doing each time, her reply was consistent: "Self-service from morning till night!"

We all stared in awe at the photographs on Mildred's bedroom wall: an autographed picture of her shaking hands with President and Lady Bird Johnson, a picture of Jacqueline Kennedy also signed, and numerous other photos of Mildred with Washington celebrities. It was overwhelming at times to think about the rich lives that had brought these people to the present. Our time spent with them connected us with the world, past and present, in new and personal ways. They helped us understand the impact of events in our own lives as they described what they had been through as children and younger adults.

During our last visit with Sam, he gently pulled me aside and said, "I just love seeing these children's smiling faces. And I love the bright, cheerful clothes they wear. We had nothing like that when we were children growing up in Russia." In that moment I had a glimpse into the hardships and struggles that contributed to the making of this incredible man. Having the opportunity to know people like Sam helped us to see the blessings of our own lives and realize that even in the face of old age and poor health it is possible to still enjoy life. As we compared Sam with other residents, less cheerful or satisfied with their life in the nursing home, we became aware that the way the elderly live could be improved. We began to think about a better vision for the elderly in the future.

Our lives were touched in many ways by our experience at the nursing home. We were impressed with the lives our elderly friends had lived—and we were equally touched by their deaths. During our two years of nursing home visits, as one might expect, several of the residents died. Our class was most deeply affected by the lives and deaths of three men: Wistano, Boot, and Sam.

Wistano

Wistano was 104 when we met him. He had paper-thin delicate skin and spoke only Spanish. During our first visits, he would peek around the corner of the room in his wheelchair, grinning at the children but too shy to come in to be with us. When Cecelia, our student teacher from Ecuador, joined us midway through first grade, she became the bridge between Wistano and the children. They would gather around him beside Cecelia and she would translate. On one occasion she told us that Wistano said he felt surrounded by angels when the children were there. His face radiated with joy sitting beside that band of angels. The children were planning a gala event for his 105th birthday, but a few weeks before, we received news that he had passed away on Easter morning. The children were all saddened by the news of the loss of this special friend but were glad that he died peacefully without suffering. Denise wrote a story about Wistano at the end of the year that summarized all our feelings about him as seen in Figure 3–1.

Boot

Boot was a great storyteller. He would always show up for our visits, sporting a baseball cap and his turquoise bolo tie. He charmed us all with tales of flying fighter planes, winning battles, and other assorted tales, including how he got his nickname. Boot was a talker, and the

```
            Wistano
         by Denise Davey

    One of the times we were at the nursing home
I talked to Wistano most of the time. Then we
went to school. The next time we went to the
nursing home Wistano died. I thought Wistano
died on a plain old day but Mary told me Wis-
tano died on Easter day.
    About every time we went to the nursing home
I talked to Wistano. But now I can't talk to
him anymore in life. Wistano was my favorite
resident because lots of kids at my mom's
school speak Spanish and he spoke Spanish. I
can talk to Wistano in my heart because that's
his spirit.
```

FIGURE 3–1   *Denise's story about Wistano*

children loved to converse with him. He had an amusing dry sense of humor, which he never held back.

During the summer when we couldn't stay away, even though the regularly scheduled school visits had ended, we surprised Boot with a birthday party. He was brought to tears by gifts, hugs, and chocolate cake. He appreciated our friendship and weekly took us down to his room to show off his photo albums and country western music collection.

Sam

Sam, like Boot, was a good storyteller. His best stories were about escaping from Russia during his boyhood. He also shared many tales related to his Jewish heritage, which delighted the children. Jenny noticed his colorful stocking hat that he wore during Hanukkah (and other days as well). She commented one day that Sam was wearing his "harmonica hat." This humorous observation led us to further discussions about Jewish holidays and traditions.

Although Sam was hard of hearing, he and the children had no difficulty communicating. The children adored him and were very distressed when his health took a turn for the worse. Even on days when he was cranky and not in the mood to see anyone, we would go to his room for quiet visits. On most days he would arise to the occasion and bring out his candy supply for his young friends. The children were almost always able to cheer him up.

Boot and Sam died within a day of each other just a few weeks after we made our informal summer visits. Like Wistano, they both went peacefully in their sleep without pain or suffering. One of the most difficult tasks I faced on our first day back in second grade was telling the children this news. I read Alice Walker's *To Hell with Dying* and then broke the news to them. We all cried and shared our favorite memories of Boot and Sam. We also reminded ourselves how fortunate we had been to have touched their lives. Although we would feel their absence, we felt blessed to have known them. Even in their dying they brought a new kind of life to our own.

Buddies

It is 9:15, and we hear a shuffle of footsteps outside our classroom door. Denise jumps up and says, "Our buddies are here!" Upon hearing the announcement of our reading buddies' weekly arrival, all the children rush to their cubbies to retrieve the books they have carefully selected and practiced the night before. Buddies find each other, some reluctantly and others with generous hugs. There is a scramble for pillows, private reading spots on the floor, and chairs at convenient tables. Through experience Jessica knows that Jordan listens better at the table. She carefully chooses a table where there will be a minimum of distractions and lays out the books she has selected. She has chosen cat books since she knows he loves cats. They settle in at the table and begin to read. In another part of the room, J. J. and Marcy snuggle up on the floor. J. J. quickly becomes so engrossed in reading the book that he doesn't realize Marcy is looking elsewhere as she sucks her thumb. I approach them and help to redirect her attention by suggesting he hold the book in front of her. In another corner, behind the bookshelf, I hear uproarious laughter. I peek around the shelf and discover Maureen and Eva, huddled together on a pillow, howling over *The Stupids Step Out*. Maureen adds humor to the story by using funny voices that tickle Eva. Tara and Sean notice the commotion and can't resist joining them.

After fifteen minutes or so, when attention spans are about to give out, we ring the bell, collect books, and gather together for a story. Today's selection is *Mrs. Cat Hides Something*. Adults and children alike are entertained by this delightful story about a mother cat, her kittens, and the kittens' father, Mr. Tom Cat. When we reach the not-so-surprising conclusion of the story, there are a few comments before good-byes are said and buddies go their separate ways.

When the buddies are safely escorted back to their own classroom, we take a few minutes to process the successes and failures of the day's buddy reading. Jennifer informs us that Dana only wanted to read *her* book and didn't want to listen to the book Jennifer had prepared. We question her about how she handled the problem, and she tells us that she read Dana's first, thinking that Dana would listen better. It didn't work. So we offer suggestions for next time and move on to Noah, who tells us how much Cheyenne enjoyed *Where's Waldo?* Our conversation is concluded by a few more success stories as we move on to the next event of the day.

Our buddies, like the nursing home residents, hadn't come into our lives by chance. The pairing of older children with younger ones for the purpose of reading had become somewhat of a school tradition several years prior. The program was started initially to promote reading across age groups. We knew it would give the older child a chance to practice reading, taking into consideration the younger child's interests and level of development. At the same time, we believed the arrangement would foster a love of reading in the younger child as a result of a positive experience with an older child. Each class in the school was paired with another class. We just happened to be matched with the three-year-olds. It turned out to be a perfect situation for all of us, and both classes looked forward to the weekly time together. The age difference was a key factor in the program's success; the three-year-olds were young enough to still want and need nurturing, and our class was old enough to do just that.

Our relationships with our buddies helped us to be compassionate and caring but in different ways than we were with our older friends at the nursing home. With the residents our job was to be ambassadors of good cheer. The children were like grandchildren to the elders. We came into their lives to fill a void created by institutions, poor health and/or old age, and family situations that often excluded them. We became their friends so we could learn more about how some elderly people spend the final years of their lives.

With the buddies the children took on more of an older sibling role. The children in our class served as teachers to their younger counterparts, guiding them in the ways of the world as well as being models for literate behavior. They took this responsibility very seriously and took pride in their buddies' progress. Jessie described her feelings about her buddy Russell in her article for the school newspaper. (See Figure 3–2.)

Although the primary intent of buddy reading was to promote a love for reading and literature, the pairing arrangement became valuable for additional purposes and extended into other aspects of school life. As time neared for the annual winter solstice performance, our two classes collaborated on a production of *The Month Brothers*, an old Slavic tale.

Emily was brilliant at stage managing Marcy, Sarah, Eva, and Dana, the three-year-old dancing flowers. She helped them feel comfortable enough to dance on stage in front of over 300 admiring parents and guests. This feeling of comfort within the buddy relationship came in handy in other ways as well. On more than one occasion, Jessica arranged a game of hide-and-seek for three-year-old Jordan when he was having difficulty separating from his mother in the morning. Jessica thoughtfully included both children from our class as well as several of Jordan's friends from his own class. There were times when the older buddy was even more successful than staff members in alleviating the anxieties of occasional upsetting events.

The sibling-like nature of the buddy relationship was especially important for those children, younger or older, who were the only child in a family. It allowed children to have special people in their lives who were also children and more than just friends.

Whenever special events came up, buddies were always consid-

Our Buddies
by Jessie Wenz

Our buddies are three years old. We work with
Sandi's class. My buddy is Russell. He used to run
around the room. Now he just sits there. He likes
trains and machines. They come on Friday morning.
It is fun to be the older buddy.

FIGURE 3–2 *Jessie's description of her buddy Russell*

ered. During special holidays we shared celebrations with our buddies
that included an exchange of cards and treats. One afternoon before
the winter holidays our buddies came to our class to share some good
cheer. We sat together around a large table and toasted our buddies
and each other with glasses of sparkling cider.

One day our class had so much fun during a science experience
with bubbles that some of the children thought it would be fun to do
bubbles with our buddies. On the next available spring morning we
abandoned our regularly scheduled plan and did "buddy bubbles." It
was a sight to behold, bubbles of all shapes and sizes, created and enjoyed by bubblers big and small. Children participated in varying de-
grees. Some of the little ones huddled together in awe as Noah
demonstrated his expertise at making gigantic six-foot bubbles. Still

others became literally immersed in it, covering themselves from head to toe in soap suds. It was one of those unforgettable experiences that had to be repeated several times before the end of the school year.

The last time we did bubbles was our final buddy celebration. To close the experience with our three-year-old friends, the children decided on a mud and sand day together. The children all wore their bathing suits and brought beach towels to school. After a morning of making bubbles, spraying each other with the hose, and creating elaborate waterways in the flooded sand pile, the buddies dried themselves off together in the Arizona sun. It was a perfect ending for these special friendships. Later on, after all the water had soaked into the desert sand, we sang together—expressing through song what we couldn't put into words. As a final last-day-of-school tribute, our now four-year-old buddies each presented their special friend from our class with a flower. It was their way of saying thank you for being a part of our lives.

Scholarly Pursuits

4

Life streamed into our classroom through the people we met. Our buddies and the residents at the nursing home, as well as others who randomly filtered in and out of our days, became a part of our circle of friends as they shared their lives with ours. They became a valuable part of our community and helped us to grow as a group and as individuals. Another important way we extended our learning was through the various studies we pursued together. Our studies often grew out of shared interests and class discussions. Sometimes I chose the study, and at other times selection was left completely up to the children. It became a joint venture in curriculum development.

Whenever possible, we tried to tie our scholarly pursuits to real life. If a world event needed attention, we studied it. When interest arose concerning a particular period of history, we explored it. As we came to know our new friends at the nursing home with their special needs, we realized that we needed more information about the aging process. So naturally, one of our first studies centered on aging and the elderly.

Intergenerational Inquiries

To better prepare ourselves for interacting with the nursing home residents, we began our first-grade year with a study of life cycles and human growth and development. We started where we were by looking at our current perceptions about the aging process. We listed what the children already knew about old people. Among the thoughts were as follows:

- their skin gets wrinkly
- sometimes they have to go in wheelchairs
- they walk slower and crooked
- they're not rich but some are
- they can't run but some can
- some need false teeth
- witches are old
- some die but some don't (e.g., Santa)

In addition to the children's current knowledge about aging, we also listed questions we had about the aging process. These lists covered the walls of our room, and we used them for many purposes, one of which was to compile pages for a class book called *The ABC's of Being Old*.

To make the book, we made a list of words for each letter of the alphabet that described older people. We listed the words and later made a sentence using one or more of them. For example, the words we came up with for "G" were *gray* hair and *glasses*, so the sentence for the book became "Some people have *gray* hair and wear *glasses* when they get old." On the day we were thinking of ideas for the "N" page, the only word anyone could come up with for "N" was "nice." We were trying to decide if there were anything else we could add to it. No one was completely satisfied with just writing "Old people are *nice*." The children knew that in some instances this was not a true statement. Ben suddenly became very animated, as he so often did when he had a brilliant idea, and shouted, "Nasty! How about nasty? Some old people can get really nasty!" We compromised by writing "Some old people are nice and some are nasty."

At this point, it seemed important to take a closer look at the stages of human development. We identified the following categories: babies, children, teenagers, young adults, middle age adults, and elders. As a lead-in to the various stages of development, I had the children work in small groups to make a chart of the characteristics of each stage. Their task was to cut pictures out of magazines that depicted humans at their assigned stage of development as well as list the characteristics they knew. To make it more interesting, I assigned the children to groups according to their experiences. For instance, children who had baby siblings worked on the baby stage. The impassioned group who lived with teenagers had, by far, the most to say about this stage of human development. They quickly filled one large piece of chart paper and begged for another. Their chart ended up being the most detailed of all the groups—and the funniest. (See Figure 4–1.)

The charts and talk about human development led us to the inevitable final stage of life, old age. We wrote and talked and read about how older people live, what they do with their time, how their bodies change. As a class we developed a survey to ask parents or grandparents how they felt about the aging process. The survey included questions such as How do you feel about getting older? Do you like having your skin get loose? How did your hair change since

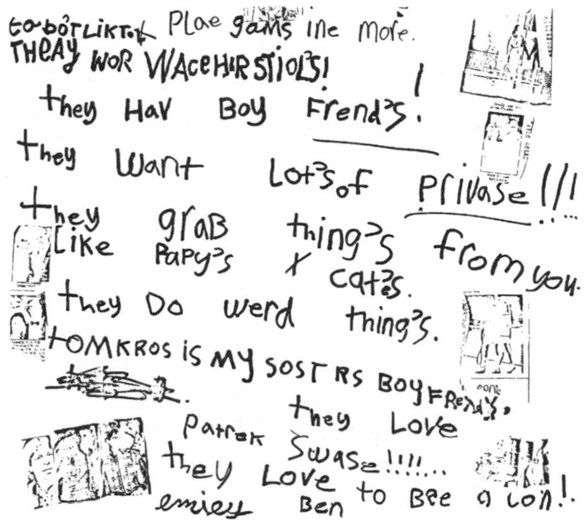

The handwritten text reads (with the typed transcription alongside):

taobotliktok Plae gams ine more.
THeAY wor WACeHIRSTIolS!
they HaV Boy Frend's.
they Want Lot's of PriVase //1
they graB thing's from you
Like PaPy's r cat's.
they Do werd thing's.
tOMKRos is My sosTRs BoyFReny,
they Love
Patrek Swase!!!!
they Love to Bee a Lon!.
emies Ben

They don't like to play games
anymore.
They wear whacky hair styles!
They have boyfriends!
They want lots of privacy!!!
They grab things from you
like puppies and cats.
They do weird things.
Tom Cruise is my sister's boyfriend.
They love Patrick Swayze!!!!!!
They love to be alone.
(by Emily, Ben and Jessie)

FIGURE 4–1 *Development chart for teenagers*

you were little? Results were sorted and categorized, enabling us to see patterns in their responses.

One of the questions that came up in a discussion was Why do you get shorter when you get older? This led to a whole study of the skeleton that eventually uncovered the answer to the question. Other questions and answers arose in our effort to understand what it might be like to be old. This quest for information continued throughout the two years we spent with the residents as we interviewed them about their age, their families, and their personal histories. The questions pertaining to human body changes that surfaced at the beginning of first grade became the foundation for an entire study of body systems in second grade.

A Systematic Approach

Building on the considerable interest the year before, I thought studying the human body would also be a good starting point for our second year of work with the elderly. A study of the body could lead to further research into the diseases of aging and the kinds of things we could do as young people to prevent those diseases from occurring. As usual, the human body study brought many surprises.

31

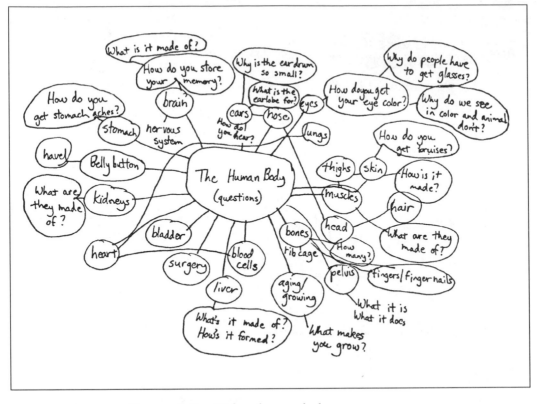

FIGURE 4–2   *Web on human body*

Initially we talked about cells and systems. We read and drew diagrams on large chart paper to try to understand what a cell is, what the parts are, and how it works. This information helped us later on as we explored the multiple systems of the human body. To broaden our study, we brainstormed what we knew about the body, creating a web. (See Figure 4–2.) We included questions we had about the body as well as our existing knowledge.

The web allowed us to sort out and name the different body systems, which teams of children then signed up to research. Once assignments were made, our classroom quickly filled up with books about the human body. The search for knowledge was on. Each team had its own collection of books specific to the assigned body system. The children carefully examined their collections of books, marking pages on which they found relevant information. Each group came up with five or more questions they thought would be important to an-

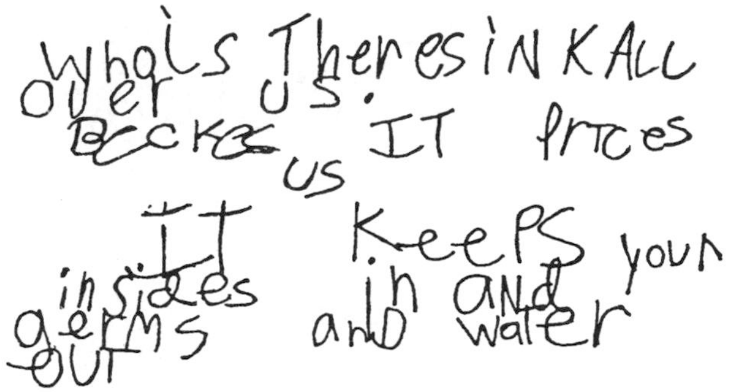

> Why is there skin all over us?
> Because it protects us. It keeps
> your insides in and germs and
> water out.

FIGURE 4–3 *Denise and Jenny's answer*

swer through their research. They wrote their questions and then gathered data in a notebook. For example, Denise and Jenny recorded the answer to their question: Why is there skin all over us? Figure 4–3 shows their answer.

After each team collected a sufficient amount of information on their system, they began preparations for their oral presentation to the class. The presentation was to include a 15 to 20 minute talk, complete with overhead transparencies and other visual aids, and a question and answer session. When each team completed its presentation to the class, the children wrote up a summary of their system for *The Human Body Atlas* we were creating. On the day before Jessie and Caitlin were to make their presentation on the brain and nervous system, I noticed them with their freshly made transparencies, notes, and a chair back in the reading corner of our room. They were practicing for the next day. They faced the wall and used the chair an overhead projector so they'd know how and when to switch to the next transparency. They took this presentation very seriously and when it was their time to stand up before the class, they were well prepared. Jessie did most of the talking during the actual presentation, but Caitlin stood attentively by her, ready to give audiovisual assistance when needed. After filling our own brains with new information, including why the heart can't pump if the brain is dead and what a dead brain and a crazy person with a small brain look like, they fielded questions from the audience. (See Figure 4–4.) One of the children asked, "How fast do the messages travel from the brain to the endings of the

FIGURE 4–4   *Jessie and Caitlin's audiovisuals*

nerves?" Jessie was quick to reply with, "I think about 25 miles per hour." When challenged that that might not be fast enough, she revised her response: "No, actually I think it's about 50 miles per hour." This seemed to satisfy the questioner, and their presentation was complete.

The presentations were informative, enlightening, and very funny. The children paid close attention to detail, as you can see in Brian and J. J.'s transparency drawings and written report. (See Figure 4–5.) The only way I kept myself from breaking out into hysterical laughter during several of the presentations was by taking copious notes. Normally the presentation would go along smoothly, but during the question and answer period I expected just about anything to happen. And it did. Here are a few of the questions and their creative replies:

- *How does the digestive system work?* "The stomach cleans it out and grinds it up . . . then you go to the bathroom!"
- *How does the poop get its shape?* "From the shape of your anus. Different people's anuses are different shapes!"
- *Do the parts of your lungs have a name?* "Yeah, but it's too hard to pronounce."
- *What is it called when two people are trying to make a baby?* "It's called rolling around. . . . Yes, if you're stupid that's what you call it."
- *How do the sperms know how to get to the right place?* "They have little eyes so they can see where to go."

Aside from the humorous quality of their answers, I felt that it was important to leave much of their information as it was, even though some of it was inaccurate. We had discussions all along the way to clarify meanings and concepts, but I believed that because the children were so young, it was important to value their approximations at understanding content, just as I honored their attempts at conventional spelling in their writing. Their misinformation about the human body systems was also a rich source of data from which to pull future topics for clarification. It was my hope that our second-grade study would be the beginning of a life-long interest in the how the human body functions. I had faith that with maturity a more accurate understanding would follow.

As the research and presentations were going on, other projects related to the human body study sprung up. Ben proudly entered the room one Monday morning carrying a model of the human body made out of paper bags that he had constructed over the weekend. When you opened a flap and looked inside, you could see an assortment of tubes, ribbon, straws, balloons, and pieces of paper taped together representing the various systems of the body.

In addition to Ben's model, the whole class worked together to construct a life-size skeleton. The children worked in teams to create ribs, vertebrae, femurs, a skull with a movable jaw, and even the tiny phalanges. Building the skeleton became somewhat of a metaphor for what was happening to our class. Working together became a common framework that held us together as learners and became a symbol of our shared learning. Each team's part was valuable and necessary to make the skeleton whole. Furthermore, our study of systems in the human body set the stage for thinking about how our class fit into the greater assembly of human beings.

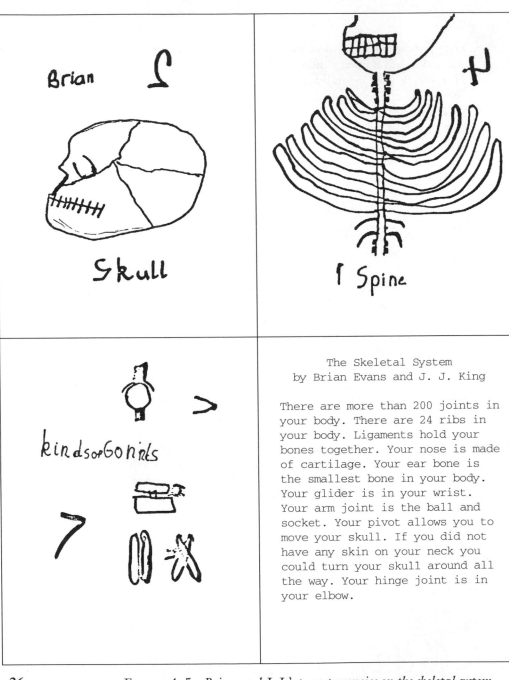

Brian

Skull

Spine

kinds of Gonnts

The Skeletal System
by Brian Evans and J. J. King

There are more than 200 joints in
your body. There are 24 ribs in
your body. Ligaments hold your
bones together. Your nose is made
of cartilage. Your ear bone is
the smallest bone in your body.
Your glider is in your wrist.
Your arm joint is the ball and
socket. Your pivot allows you to
move your skull. If you did not
have any skin on your neck you
could turn your skull around all
the way. Your hinge joint is in
your elbow.

　FIGURE 4–5　*Brian and J. J.'s transparencies on the skeletal system*

Whenever possible, we tried to see how our own lives connected to other people's. Two cultural studies we did, one on Ecuador and the other on Japan, helped us see the differences as well as the similarities between our culture and that of people in faraway countries. During the Japan study (Glover, 1990), we had special guests who taught us about the tea ceremony and how to do origami. The children did research projects on various aspects of Japanese culture such as their food, housing, animals, celebrations and festivals, and doll making. After reading about Japanese doll makers, Maureen made one of the first connections between the Japanese culture and her own when she brought in a plastic bag of her mom's cut hair. She had discovered that they used real human hair to make the dolls and thought ours should be authentic! After completing their research each team wrote a summary of their findings and did a project. A model Japanese home, authentic food, a volcano replica, and a fishing boat were among the projects featured at our open house for the parents and other children in the school. The open house celebration, which included a dance interpretation of *The Big Wave* (see Chapter 5), culminated the two-month study.

Our cultural studies helped us see the similarities and differences of people's lives within our own culture as well. We talked about how those differences have affected people historically. This led us to an examination of human and civil rights, and the individuals who dedicated their lives to helping to improve the quality of life for all humanity. Among those we investigated were Mahatma Gandhi, Martin Luther King, Jr., and Harriet Tubman.

Our study of Martin Luther King, Jr.'s life began during first grade around the time of his birthday celebration in January. We learned of Gandhi, whose ideas and practices greatly influenced King's thinking. That first year we became familiar with the events of King's life and their historical importance for all people, both black and white. One day we turned part of our classroom into a bus as we dramatized the famous Rosa Parks story and discussed how the bus boycott worked to make change. We learned about the Nobel Peace Prize and Martin Luther King, Jr.'s famous "I Have A Dream" speech. Poetry was written that captured the essence of our knowledge of King's life. (See Figure 4–6.) We sadly read of King's assassination and discussed at length why someone would want to kill a person like King, John F. Kennedy, or Mahatma Gandhi. This dia-

FIGURE 4–6 *Katie's poem about Martin Luther King, Jr.*

logue laid the groundwork for the more sophisticated study that would follow in second grade.

When a year had passed and it was again time to celebrate King's birthday, we became involved in a brief discussion of slavery. I was reading a book about the Underground Railroad that sparked the interest of the entire class. To learn more about the Railroad's history we read *Freedom Train*, the biography of Harriet Tubman. To help us keep track of dates and events we made a time line, which included

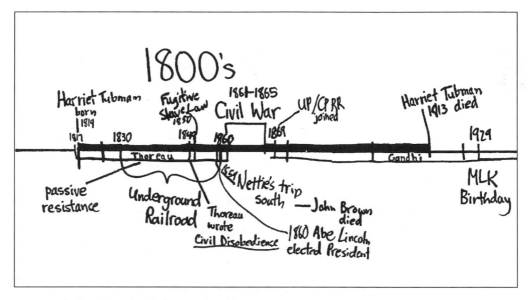

FIGURE 4–7   *Harriet Tubman time line*

the arrival of the first slaves in America, the Civil War period, and the life spans of Thoreau, Gandhi, Tubman, and King. (See Figure 4–7.) One child amusingly commented: "Isn't it interesting how everything all happened around the time of the Civil War?" He just assumed that since the time line in the mid-1880s was so full that it was the only time in history when anything happened!

With the help of our time line and a great deal of discussion, we painstakingly waded through the details of Harriet Tubman's life— just as she meticulously worked her way through enemy territory to free the slaves. We were horrified to hear about her master throwing a heavy weight at her forehead while she helped another slave run away. We learned about how she cared for wounded soldiers and risked her life time after time to help other slaves escape to freedom in the North. As we read about each act of courage, we began to recognize a pattern in her life as well as in the lives of many other human beings. Sometimes situations exist that are greater than people's personal lives and that call for them to sacrifice everything they have to preserve what they know in their hearts to be true. This became a theme in not only our reading of *Freedom Train* but in many of the other books we read together. The books we shared, sometimes tied to our scholarly pursuits and sometimes not, provided us yet another avenue into the world outside our classroom.

39

5 And Jesse Was the Gate

❧ The class has just finished reading the conclusion to *Abel's Island*, the tale of a mouse who has been stranded alone on a remote island for a year away from his beloved wife. Some children are lying on the floor, and others are sitting up, eager to share their comments about the ending. A few of the children are not happy with how the book ends. They feel as if Steig has left them hanging and they want to know further details of Abel and Amanda's reunion. This conversation unfolds:

JENNIFER: I would be *astonished* if I was Amanda and Abel came home!

CHARLIE: I'd think Amanda would be thinking Abel was dead.

JENNIFER: I like how the author put in another adventure with the cat. He put in the risk of being eaten by the cat.

MAUREEN: He really built it up, one adventure after the other.

JESSIE: I'd think Amanda would've been married too. It would have been hard for Abel if he walked in and Amanda was with another man.

BEN: Especially if they were kissing!

MARY: Why do you think she didn't marry another mouse?

JESSICA: I think she believed he was alive somewhere.

NOAH: She had that thing in her mind that she knew what he was doing (ESP).

JENNIFER: Steig could have had Amanda say, "Will you promise to never do this again?" And then they would go out.

EMILY: The ending's like a hill, and it doesn't let you know it's going to end, and then you fall off.

J. J.: It's a cliff hanger. You fall down where it suddenly ends, and then you start all over with a new story.

BEN: It should be the new series of a romance catalogue!

For the most part, our scholarly pursuits broadened our knowledge base and enabled us to connect with the world. Through our studies we were able to see how the life we lived in our classroom fit into the greater scheme of things. As our minds were being enriched through scholarly interests, our hearts were being educated primarily through literature. In fact, the literary journey we took together often functioned as a bridge between the heart and the mind. As we examined Steig's writing style, we also came to understand the depth and range of feeling between two individuals who loved each other.

Books were an integral part of our classroom. Since the very beginning of my teaching career, I've believed that it's difficult to teach if you don't know books. Consequently I've spent hundreds of hours hanging around bookstores and libraries, as well as talking to other teachers and friends about children's books. I've made it a habit of writing down titles I hear about for later reference. Although I have tried to use the library as much as possible, I've built up my own library over the years. Along with my own books and those in our classroom library, children and their parents would often bring in favorites from home or the library, particularly if they related to our current study. We also accumulated books from book clubs, used book sales, and children who had outgrown their books at home. Books were highly respected and valued. We used them in the following ways:

- *Content Study Work* Books such as *Tales of a Gambling Grandma, Nana Upstairs and Nana Downstairs, Knots on a Counting Rope*, and *Now One Foot, Now the Other* were used for our study of aging and the elderly.
- *General Information and Research Books* Such books as the Eyewitness Book *Skeleton* or *Why Do Our Bodies Stop Growing?* were used for specific topics.
- *Independent Reading* Children chose any book they were interested in reading silently for approximately a half hour daily.
- *Just for Fun* These were mostly picture books that became class favorites like *Miss Nelson Is Missing, The Stupids Step Out, Two Bad Ants*, and *Where the Wild Things Are*—read for pure enjoyment and a dose of humor.
- *Read Aloud/Whole Group Literature Study* These were usually longer books with a myriad of opportunities for dialogue such as *Sarah, Plain and Tall, Dominic, Abel's Island, Julie of the Wolves*, and *Tuck Everlasting*. They were read to the whole group and discussed afterwards.
- *Small Group Literature Study* A group of four to six children (and a teacher) would read the same book or related

Figure 5–1   *Miss Swamp joke*

books and meet several times to share responses to their reading.

Loads of Laughter

In previous chapters, I discussed how we used books for our content studies and for obtaining general information. Our experiences with literature just for fun and enjoyment, both independently and as a group, were equally important. Of course we had our favorite authors and books. James Marshall and Harry Allard were high on the list with their notable characters—the Stupids, Miss Nelson, and the relentless Miss Viola Swamp. Miss Swamp became a permanent member of our circle and was the subject of numerous poems and jokes (See Figure 5–1.)

We were all fans of Chris Van Allsburg's work, in particular *Jumanji*, *The Garden of Abdul Gasazi*, and *Two Bad Ants*. Anthony Browne's *Willy the Wimp* was always good for an uproarious laugh when we turned the page and saw him admiring himself in the mirror (in his pumped-up condition) thinking he "liked what he saw." Frog and Toad, two lively characters created by Arnold Lobel, were as much a part of our literary circle as members of our own class. They came up in humorous conversations along with members of William Steig's adventuresome crew of talking donkeys, dogs, cats, and mice.

On one occasion I overheard Mia and Ben chattering away as they were painting a jungle mural. They were discussing strategies for getting the microscopic details of a leaf on their paper:

BEN: I went to an arting [sic] class once where they showed us a one-haired paint brush!

MIA: Remember like in *Dominic* where Dominic tried to sniff that rose because he thought it was real but it was a painting?

BEN: Yes, that rose had the veins in it.

MIA: Every single one.

These storybook friends not only provided nourishment to our collective sense of humor, but they also became reference points for more serious literary dialogue and critique.

A Circle of Critics

It's early in our first-grade year, and I've just finished reading *Two Bad Ants*. We spend a considerable amount of time talking about perspective and point of view since the text and illustrations are presented from the ants' point of view. For example, a cup of coffee is referred to as a hot brown lake of "terrible, bitter water." We come up with this chart:

Two Bad Ants
(point of view)

human	*ants*
sugar	crystals
coffee	lake of bitter water
grass	forest
mouth	cave
wall	mountain
faucet	waterfall
garbage disposal	chamber
bread	disks
electric shock	strange force
side of the cup	shore

A few months later, in a small group literature study of *Frog and Toad All Year*, Ben, Emily, and Noah discuss an illustration in the story "Ice Cream." The picture shows Toad walking along with a big blob of brown ice cream all over him and two pointed objects on his head. Emily insists that "in real life he wouldn't actually look that way." Ben becomes very animated and replies, "Oh yes, he would! It's like . . . what was that thing from *Two Bad Ants*? . . . uh, point of view! Yes, from Toad's point of view that's what it would be like to have an ice cream cone on your head." To prove the point further he constructs a life-size toad and ice cream cone out of playdough and then plops the cone on the toad's head. It is nearly an identical replica of the illustration.

Careful examination of the writing styles of our favorite authors also made us pay more attention to writing as a craft. We began to see and hear literature from a more critical perspective. In a study of Steig's work, we discussed *Dominic*. We looked at the words Steig used to describe how Dominic was feeling during one part of the story. We came upon words like "doldrums," "dreary," and "dumps" and talked about how they all mean sad or depressed. Noah commented, "It's neat how the author uses different words to say the same thing but doesn't just use plain old words." Another time, while exchanging impressions of James Howe's writing of *Bunnicula*, Ben noted, "The way he uses words gives you a big *burst* of what's happening."

Our work with literature in both large and small groups was extensive and varied. Some books were enjoyed for their splendid language, such as *Dr. DeSoto's* comment about the fox in the dental chair: "The fox had a rotten bicuspid and unusually bad breath." Other books, *When I Was Young in the Mountains*, for example, became favorites for the imagery they evoked: "When I was young in the mountains, Grandfather came home in the evening covered with the black dust of a coal mine. Only his lips were clean, and he used them to kiss the top of my head." A few titles, like Sendak's *Outside Over There*, always kept us intrigued and filled with wonder even after repeated readings.

Different books met the needs and interests of individuals at different times. There were moments when a certain book would make a profound impression on a child. Charlie kept returning to *Fox in Love* again and again because he loved the humor in it. I could find him on almost any given day, chuckling over Fox and his self-created troubles with his multiple girlfriends. Maureen and Mia grabbed *The Facts of Life* every spare moment they had because it had been one of their primary resource books in their human body research. Jessica devoured any Laura Ingalls Wilder book she could get her hands on. *Bunnicula* was popular with many of the children after reading it aloud, and it was difficult to find a James Howe book on the shelf for months afterward. Some books simply made individual children come alive. But during the two years there were three books we read together that made a lasting impression on our class, leaving all of our minds and hearts forever changed.

The Big Wave

Midway through first grade we embarked on our study of Japan. To get the study going I decided to read a few Japanese folktales and then took a chance on a longer story, Pearl Buck's *The Big Wave*. It was one of my favorites, and although I thought it might be a challenge for the class, I wanted to try it as our first long read aloud. The book is about two Japanese boys and a tidal wave that alters the course of both their lives. Before the end of the first day we had already begun a list of character differences between Kino, the farmer's son, and Jiya, the fisherman's son. The children began to discern the theme of the book: Enjoy life, don't fear death.

Each day when I read they would beg me not to stop. The dialogue was rich and meaningful. One time as we talked about why the ocean was so deep around Kino and Jiya's island, Ben theorized, "It's at the back of the ocean. There's a front and a back, and it's at the back." Further negotiation of meaning helped us to understand that the steep-sided island was formed by a volcano. On the same day Ben gave his theory on the ocean, we talked about why Jiya's family sent him up the hill alone, knowing the rest of them would perish in the big wave. This was the conversation:

NOAH: Why didn't the whole family go with Jiya?
CHARLIE: Yes, they should have gone with Jiya.
NOAH: Maybe Jiya's father wanted to face his fear.

This led us to a discussion of symbolism, and we started a list of symbols in the story. Then I wrote Jiya's name on the list.

MARY: What is Jiya a symbol of?
CHARLIE: Jiya was the soul of the family. He kept it alive by living.

Our dialogue that day, and particularly Charlie's comment, opened up a new dimension of understanding. Working together to grasp the meaning of symbolism and recognizing the depth of Charlie's words brought an unspoken sense of knowing to each and every one of us. I could see it in the children's faces.

From that day on the dialogue became richer and the comments more powerful. When we talked about how life became more precious after the big wave, Jacob reflected, "Life is like glass breaking. If it broke you'd be sorry because you spent a lot of money on it." In other words, Jiya's life was shattered. We realized how each of our lives is just as vulnerable and easily broken. We continued talking about how life appears more valuable when you live in danger. Jessie offered, "When you live with danger you're not afraid." Caitlin then added, "It gives you the chance to have enough braveness so you can live a long time."

Reluctantly we finished *The Big Wave*. We wrote and illustrated poetry about the book and performed it as a dance for parents and friends. *The Big Wave* stayed in our hearts for a long time. Somehow because we understood what Jiya symbolized, we lived and breathed the story more fully. We felt his pain when he lost his family and his courage in the face of this loss. Because we had come to know Jiya together, we could all be more brave—in sharing ideas and in living.

Tuck Everlasting

About a year later we read *Tuck Everlasting*. Natalie Babbitt tells the story of the Tuck family who by chance discovers and drinks a special kind of water that gives them life everlasting. The situation becomes complicated when eleven-year-old Winnie Foster ventures out of her fenced-in yard one hot August day and finds the source of the water in the wood near her home. She is kidnapped by the Tucks who want the truth of the water to be kept a secret so other people won't have to suffer their fate—to be removed from the wheel of life and stuck at the point in time when they drank the water. Throughout the book seventeen-year-old Jesse Tuck tries to convince Winnie to wait until she is his age, drink the water, and be his wife forever. As the story unfolds Winnie is faced with many factors to consider before making that decision.

We proceeded with our study of *Tuck*, listing the symbols as they occurred to us in the story:

- *spring water*—life not changing, life not moving
- *music box*—love, traveling
- *man in yellow*—evil, danger, trickery

- *Winnie*—growing, life, growth cycle
- *wood*—running away, adventure
- *pond*—life everlasting, life reproducing
- *boat*—the Tucks being out of the wheel of life, being trapped on Earth, not being able to go to heaven

The symbolism of Tuck continued to dominate the dialogue as we worked our way through the book. And then one morning during the writing workshop, I realized that not only were the children picking up the symbolism of the story but they were also beginning to use metaphor to tie the book to other parts of their lives. One of the third graders was in the author's chair sharing his writing with our class. He was having some problems with his lead and his ending. We discussed the importance of these parts in a piece of writing and Ben commented, "A story is kind of like a wheel too, like in *Tuck Everlasting*; it has a beginning and an end." Noah then interjected, "If you drink the water you get stuck, just like your story gets stuck." Then Ben added, "It's like his story drank the water and it got stuck. Or like people were reading the story, and the wheel was turning, and they got confused, and it got stuck."

Sitting there listening to them help a fellow writer improve his craft, I realized Noah and Ben had tapped into a community pool of metaphors that they had actively contributed to through discussions of literature. Through their participation, they were making connections between daily school events and our class study of *Tuck Everlasting*, using the metaphors to join the two. Sharing these metaphors seemed to sustain them and give them power.

I was struck by the children's ability to use metaphor. I began to examine more closely how metaphor worked with and for them. Our work with literature was the birthing ground for using metaphors, but their use was not limited to our literary discussions. During a follow-up discussion after completing a science experiment with bubbles, one of the children exclaimed, "Doing the bubbles was like a good story—they just grab you, and you want to get into it, and you don't want to put it down."

I began to see that shared metaphor grows out of talk. As learners work together to construct and reconstruct meaning through dialogue, powerful metaphors often emerge. As talk continues, metaphor is extended.

When we first started talking about the water in *Tuck*, both the spring that the Tucks drank and the water in the pond, Ben said, "It is like the cycle of life; it was like they were in a canoe that tipped over, and they fell out and couldn't get back in. It's like they were going down the tube of life, and they found a little trapdoor to get out, and they couldn't get back in." Then Jennifer proclaimed, "It seemed like the Tucks were drowning in life forever." As we continued to work the metaphors related to the water, their power grew. The classroom atmosphere became electrified as these powerful ideas poured forth.

Metaphors that arose out of spontaneous discussions became shared symbols for everyone within our circle. They were taken on as part of the community mind. The sharing gave them power and existence, and it was only through their cocreation by a group of committed learners that they came forth. They weren't preplanned or prepackaged. They arose out of the rich talk that was shared amongst all of us.

Frank Smith (1983) writes:

> Metaphors are the legs of language, on which thought steadily advances or makes its more daring leaps. Without metaphor thought is inert and with the wrong metaphor it is hobbled. Metaphors are inescapable. Language cannot address reality directly (whatever 'reality' might be without metaphor). Metaphors are the analogies by which one thing is explored or discussed in terms of another, the familiar used as a fulcrum to reveal the unknown.

The use of shared metaphor provided a unique way of knowing. Metaphor became our mutual bridge for understanding things in life that were difficult to grasp. It became a tool for thinking and extending our knowledge. The use of metaphor enabled us to slip into new realms of thought and feeling. When we tapped into the use of metaphor, it allowed everyone to access other worlds of the mind and heart. Metaphor enabled us to go beyond words and to understand commonly shared meanings.

When we shared the work of creating metaphors, our thinking took quantum leaps. During our final discussion about *Tuck Everlasting*, we pondered the symbolic nature of the toad. Elizabeth said the toad was a part of Winnie's life, and Emily added that it was like a companion. Jessie then commented, "The toad was a symbol of not drinking the water. The toad was another side of Winnie." Maureen said, "The toad was free, he could do whatever he wanted without being bossed around. Winnie couldn't." This led us to talk about the fence around Winnie's house, and how she couldn't get out of the fence but the toad could. Jessica thoughtfully stated, "The fence was like the wheel. It kept Winnie in it. The talk with Tuck was like the fence—it kept her from getting out of the wheel. She poured the water on the toad because she knew she'd be unhappy [if she drank the water] after her talk with Tuck." Insightfully Noah reflected: "The door to the fence was open [for Winnie] to drink the water but she couldn't . . . and Jesse was the gate. But in the end the toad helped her close the gate when she poured the water on it." For Winnie, Jesse was the gate—an opening into the possibilities of a life outside time. For each of us the shared metaphor became a gate as well, a gate opening our hearts and minds to a new idea about time and about life.

Julie of the Wolves

In the springtime of second grade, we were in the midst of a study of animals. Wanting to incorporate literature into the study, Desireé, our student teacher, chose to read *Julie of the Wolves* to the class. It was difficult reading at first, and she had to reread several parts along the way to help make the meaning clear. It was a struggle to understand this story of Julie, a young Eskimo girl who runs away from home, gets lost in the Alaskan tundra, and is adopted by a pack of Arctic wolves. The descriptions of wolf behaviors and living habits made it hard to get through the book and much of the talk centered on purely trying to make sense of what was going on in the story. The book did hold the children's interest, however, and we arrived at the final passage of the book where Julie has to decide whether to return to the pack of wolves or go to live with her father Kapugen:

> She sang to the spirit of Amaroq [the head of the wolf pack] in her best English:
>
> The seals are scarce and the whales are almost gone.
> The spirits of the animals are passing away.
> Amaroq, Amaroq, you are my adopted father.
> My feet dance because of you.
> My eyes see because of you.
> My mind thinks because of you. And it thinks, on
> this thundering night,
> That the hour of the wolf and the Eskimo is over.
>
> Julie pointed her boots toward Kapugen.

When Desireé finished reading I asked, "Why did Julie point her boots toward Kapugen?" The question ignited a dialogue that spread like wildfire around our circle. Their responses to the question were remarkable:

ELIZABETH: She was in the middle of the life that was behind her and the life that was ahead of her. If she decided to go back it would be with the wolves. If she decided to go forward she would go to her father. She decided to walk forward.

JESSIE: She needed human love. If she went back it'd be like [living] a re-run.

TARA: Yes, her wolf life was over. She needed a human being.

EMILY: She wished she had two lives. She wanted the wolves and she wanted her father. She knew that the wolves were in the past and that couldn't be changed.

JENNIFER: It's like this school—when we leave here we'll miss this school a whole ton. But we have to leave when it's time.

Our talk moved on as Desireé commented, "Life is like a chapter in a book; one chapter comes to an end but there is always a new one waiting to be read." Jennifer then made a statement about how our lives all fit together that set off more dialogue:

EMILY: Julie's life was like a puzzle. When she's just about to die the picture becomes clear. She realizes that she has to live all those pieces.

JESSIE: Julie working with the wolves is just like us all working together. What Caitlin said gave me ideas and that helped everyone.

ELIZABETH: It was like Julie had a puzzle out all her life and she would put one more piece onto the puzzle each year. [When she got older] she would ask her children to help her finish it. You make a puzzle when you're born.

EMILY: It gets clearer and clearer each year.

JESSIE: Yeah, and we're all joined together in peace to make the big puzzle. The picture won't be complete until we're all put together.

In that moment, as I looked at the openness of their wise young faces, I knew we had experienced the essence of dialogue. A clarity and a commitment to our work and each other was present as it had never been before. At one point I stopped the exchange of words and asked everyone to pay close attention to what was going on. I asked them to notice how ideas were flowing in and out of each other and how we were all getting smarter in our thinking because of the way we were working together. Even though they couldn't verbalize it, I knew they understood. They knew that sitting there in our circle, talking about a fine piece of literature, we had added a few more pieces to the puzzle and had come closer to completing the picture.

6 Tookies, Trains, and Terrible Twos

✎ Before Thanksgiving I had to be gone a few days to a conference in Baltimore. I left my lively second graders with Michael, their favorite substitute. When I returned I was greeted with a collection of letters. Maureen's was among them. (See Figure 6–1.) I was pleased with her informative update of the class's progress while I was away and appreciated her filling me in on the important details of her own life. Maureen, along with the rest of her classmates, understood the potency of being a writer. The children had come to this realization through their study of literature and through careful attention paid to the many uses of print in our lives. They learned that writing is an effective means of communication when talk can't serve our needs. Maureen knew the message she couldn't convey to me in person would be communicated in print. She and her classmates figured out that a message intended for many people or one that needed to be preserved over a period of time could best be shared through writing. They understood that the need to share thoughts with someone far away or to express feelings too private to say out loud could be met through writing.

Writing became the visible documentation of life in our classroom. Signs were posted around the room to remind people of important events. Our classroom was filled with the charts we had written as a group and our bookshelves were lined with titles authored by individual children. Issues of *The Seed News*, the school newspaper produced by our class with help from writers in other classrooms, circulated into the hands of all interested readers—friends and family alike. Letters were mailed off to Maine and Japan with great anticipation of the replies. Journals were kept and scientific data were recorded. Sometimes writing was a solitary venture with children writing alone. At other times children chose to write collaboratively in teams. Always there was writing and always it was for a purpose.

Writing Workshop

We had a designated block of time for writing workshop each day

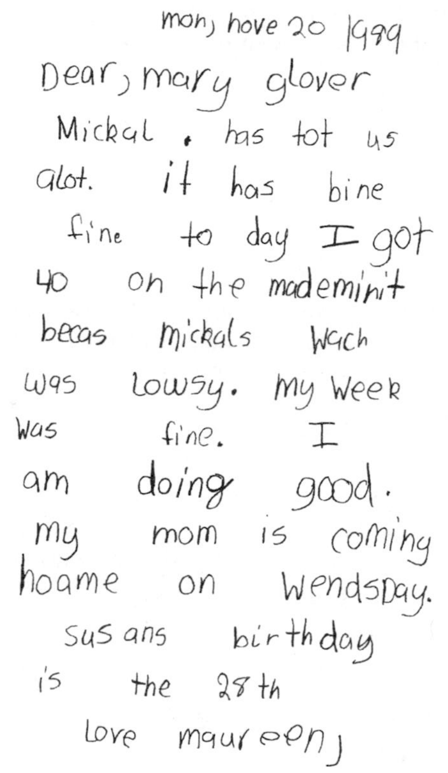

> mon, hove 20 1989
> Dear, mary glover
> Mickal . has tot us
> alot. it has bine
> fine to day I got
> 40 on the mademinit
> becas mickals wach
> was lowsy. my week
> was fine. I
> am doing good.
> my mom is coming
> hoame on wendsDay.
> susans birthday
> is the 28th
> love maureenj

Dear Mary Glover,
Michael has taught us a
lot. It has been fun.
Today I got 40 on the
Mad Minute because
Michael's watch was
lousy. My week was fine.
I am doing good. My
mom is coming home on
Wednesday. Susan's
birthday is the 28th.
Love, Maureen

FIGURE 6–1 *Maureen's letter*

that usually lasted about an hour to an hour and a half. The type of writing going on varied according to what was happening in the classroom at the time. For example, during our first-grade study of Japan, most of the writing workshop time was devoted to taking notes, writing letters, and writing reports. When we completed our study of Martin Luther King, Jr., we spent several days writing poetry. When we studied animals, the time was used to write scripts for puppet shows. One day when Denise lost the stitch from her dog she had brought to school in an envelope, she used her time to write a letter to the dog's vet requesting another stitch. Sometimes we'd use writing workshop for writing letters to our pen pals so we could get them in the mail by a certain date. Much of the time during writing workshop was available for individual children to pursue their own interests. Regardless of the content, the writing workshop had its ritual:

- *Mini-lesson*   It might be a short lesson on spelling or punctuation or involve reading a book to model good leads, endings, description.
- *Silent writing*   Quiet, solitary writing (no talk) for 10 to 15 minutes
- *General writing*   Writing, illustrating, conferring with teacher or other writers, revising, editing, gathering ideas for topics, and so on.
- *Author sharing*   One or more children share a piece they are working on to get feedback, assistance, or clarification from the class. When a book has been published, this time is used for celebration as the child reads it to the group

Writing workshop was filled with talk as well as writing. Aside from the silent writing period, children were free to speak with others, ask for help, and solicit opinions. Often a writer would request a conference with me or with another student. It took time and practice to be a good listener—and to make suggestions that would help a fellow writer grow. Eavesdropping on conferences became one of my favorite pastimes during writing workshop when I wasn't busy conferring with someone:

JENNIFER TO TARA AFTER READING HER PIECE: Trust me, it makes sense!

MAUREEN'S CONFERENCE WITH MIA: Wait, Mia, you're mixing me up!

MIA: That's what I'm here for!

JACOB HELPING NOAH ON HIS SPACE STORY: You need to have more about the trip back. You don't say anything about the trip home.

NOAH: Jacob, you know that nothing ever happens on the way back [when you go on a trip]!

BEN (CHIMING IN): Well, doesn't he have a little radio or something he could listen to?

JENNIFER TO EMILY DISCUSSING A CHARACTER IN HER PIECE: "In the old days they [women] didn't have jobs. All they did was clean and have babies . . . and be queens. And bow to kings!"

I never knew what to expect from writing workshop. Each day was different and had some spontaneity to it. Some days were so filled with outstanding effort that we all felt highly energized at the end of the workshop. At other times, it was just plain hard work, and we were glad to move on to something else. Almost every day provided at least one writing workshop story to share with other teachers. Among my favorites was the day Adrin came up to me and asked if I'd "sterilized" her story yet. She had given it to me the day before, requesting that I edit it for her. There was also Jennifer's comment on revision: "If you're in a good mood, it's not hard, and it makes your story better."

Regardless of the unpredictability of each writing workshop, there were specific categories of writing that surfaced throughout the course of our two years together. It is worth noting that many of these kinds of writing also happened at other times of the day besides during the writing workshop.

True-life Stories

It made sense to start with personal narrative in first grade. The theory was that writing about something that actually happened would be easier than writing fiction because you'd know the details you'd need to include in your piece. Most of the children stayed with personal narrative for their individual writing well into second grade. Charlie wrote a touching story of his grandmother's dog Sammy who had died. We had Emily's dog trilogy and Tara's exciting adventure, *Barbara the Bucking Elephant*, which tells of the near mishap she and her small cousin had while riding a circus elephant. Jessica informed us of the problems of borrowed ski equipment as she retold the story of her aunt's skiing accident. Denise had everyone on the floor in hysterics when she read *Taxi, Madame?*, her true-life tale of a taxi driver in Egypt who had black teeth. Jenny wrote of her family's favorite pastime, bowling. And Caitlin authored an amusing account of her little brother Richie called *Terrible Twos*. We could all appreciate this delightful story about one of our class's favorite (and frequent) visitors! She captured both the frustrations and the joys of having a two-year-old brother. (See Figure 6–2.)

One special collection of true-life stories was the memoirs the children wrote during second grade. Noah's *Funny Things Always Happen* included an account of the day he tripped over someone's violin case at a music institute in Utah and splattered cherry pie all over himself. In *The Untold Story of Emily Thomas' Life*, Emily describes

Usually he is pretty cheerful before bed but he starts to
cry in bed. He is in the terrible twos. It's hard to get
along with him sometimes. I think twos are the worst so far.

FIGURE 6–2   *Caitlin's story about her little brother*

her early preschool experience: "When I was three I learned the alphabet. When I was four I went to the Seed, not to mention having my first book published." Jenny, who was born on her mom's thirtieth birthday, described herself as her mom's favorite birthday present in *When I Was Born*. In Mia's memoir *Young Stories and Funny Things*, she describes her first communications in detail: "My first language was tongue talking. My dad would stick his tongue out and after that I would stick my tongue out once or twice. This started out when I was a baby." Jessica included a swimming lesson experience in her memoir. (See Figure 6–3.) The memoirs not only served as a written document of each child's life but also brought a greater sense of appreciation for each other to our class. By sharing our histories we each shared a bit more of ourselves.

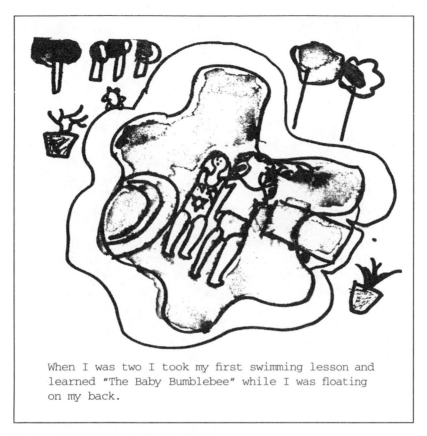

When I was two I took my first swimming lesson and
learned "The Baby Bumblebee" while I was floating
on my back.

FIGURE 6–3 *From Jessica's memoir*

It was not unusual for some of the true life stories to have a bit
of fiction interwoven. J. J. wrote a story about his gerbil and included
an illustration of a bright red gerbil with the text: "Gerbils can only
stand 80°." When questioned about this he replied, "When gerbils
get over 80°, they turn bright red . . . all except the black ones, and I
have a black one. The black ones do live to be a hundred years old,
though!"

Maureen kept us well entertained with her book, *Two-Kid
Slumber Party*, an account of an exciting evening she and Denise
spent together. After Maureen had shared her story with the class,
Denise quietly pulled me aside and with a horrified look on her face
informed me that *none* of it was true! That provided a great lead-in
for talking about how true-life stories are often the basis for fiction.

Meet the Tookies

Like most of the children, Noah started his first grade year with personal narrative. He wrote about Herbie, the Volkswagen his mom was rebuilding in their garage, and he wrote about his two sisters. Then one day he announced that he wanted to try fiction since all his other books were true stories. He was ready for something different. His story design of *The Planet Tookie* was nearly identical to that of *Where the Wild Things Are*. I realized that through our work with literature Noah had internalized the elements of Sendak's story without copying it.

There were many parallels. First of all, his main character is a boy (with a pet), and there are no adults around until the very end of the story. The boy has a private tent, similar to Max's "private boat." The cat and the boy build a rocket ship, a vehicle to carry them off to their adventure, much like Max's boat. Noah wrote, "It took them several weeks and months"—closely resembling Sendak's line, "in and out of weeks and almost over a year." When the rocket is finished they get in. Noah's text reads, "Then the boy and his cat got in the rocket ship and counted down. 3, 2, 1 . . . BLAST OFF! They were in the air. By night they were in space." He uses almost the same transition to return them home Sendak uses at the end of *Where the Wild Things Are*: "he sailed off through the night and day and in and out of weeks and almost over a year . . ." When Noah's main characters land on the Planet Tookie, they are greeted by a pack of ten giant Tookie Eaters. They are large and friendly, and interestingly resemble Sendak's wild things. (See Figure 6–4.) After a delightful time of playing games, perhaps as enjoyable as "the wild rumpus," the boy and his cat must return home, as Max does. They say their regretful good-byes and step into their rocket. By morning they return home with breakfast on the table, just as Max's supper is waiting for him when he returns from *Where the Wild Things Are*.

Noah's story, in addition to all the fiction we were reading, served as a reference point for other fiction writers in our class. By second grade several children had moved into this genre. J. J. wrote a series of space adventures, and Brian came up with a delightfully illustrated book about a talking pencil. Maureen produced an undersea tale of a mermaid at the same time that Jennifer and Tara collaborated on a book called *Amazing Bunnies*. And by the end of second grade Noah had written *Tookies on Earth*, his sequel to *The Planet Tookie*. Fiction was alive and well in our classroom—as was poetry.

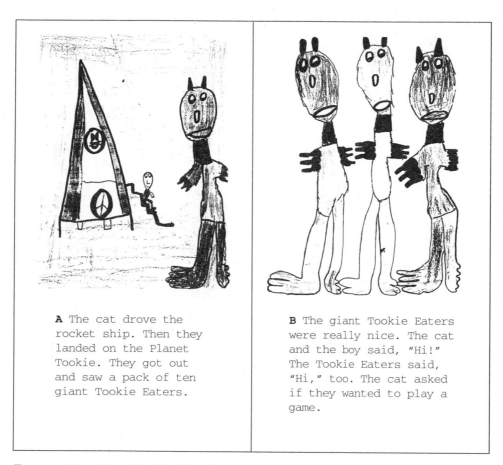

A The cat drove the rocket ship. Then they landed on the Planet Tookie. They got out and saw a pack of ten giant Tookie Eaters.

B The giant Tookie Eaters were really nice. The cat and the boy said, "Hi!" The Tookie Eaters said, "Hi," too. The cat asked if they wanted to play a game.

FIGURE 6–4   *From Noah's* The Planet Tookie

Lively Poets' Society

Writing fiction was made easier for Noah and his classmates because we read lots of fiction. Immersing children in poetry had the same effect. We became a circle of poets because we loved the imagery and sounds of poetry. Poetry, both the reading and writing of it, became a part of our daily life. *Imaginary Gardens*, *The New Kid on the Block*, *Where the Sidewalk Ends*, and *Tomie dePaola's Book of Poems* were among our favorite sources of poetry.

We read all kinds of poetry and talked about what makes a poem different from a story. It took time to understand the difference. During a discussion one day I posed the question: What is a poem? Brian replied, "It's like little peeks into the words." Ben added: "It's the voice." We talked about voice in poetry as well as

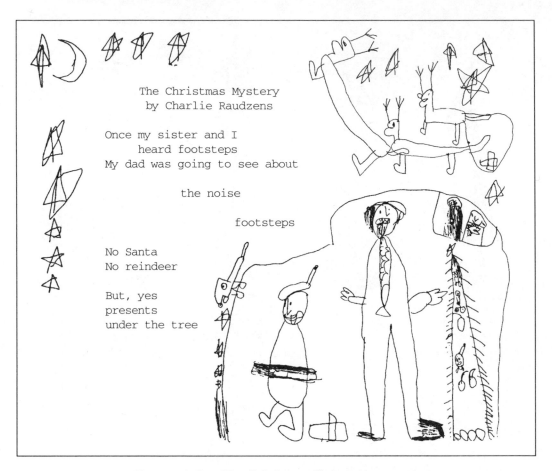

The Christmas Mystery
by Charlie Raudzens

Once my sister and I
        heard footsteps
My dad was going to see about

        the noise

                footsteps

No Santa
No reindeer

But, yes
presents
under the tree

FIGURE 6–5   *Charlie's Santa Claus poem*

repetition, sound, rhythm, and image (Heard, 1989). Before long, poetry was flowing in, around, and through our heads, filling our room with delightful verse:

Poetry Flows with the Wind
by Emily Thomas

Some poems rhyme
Some don't rhyme

Some are happy
Some are sad

Some are serious
Some are silly

Some are mad
Some are peaceful

Some are scary
Some are upright weird

Poetry flows
with the wind

Poetry flows with the wind
and belongs to the beholder

Sometimes you worry
Sometimes you don't

flows with the wind
flows with the wind

As a group, one of our first attempts at poetry was a collection of holiday verse. Charlie's poem about the mystery of Santa Claus captured the spirit of the season. (See Figure 6–5.)

With our pens still warm from the holiday poetry, we put together another collection of poems to commemorate Dr. Martin Luther King, Jr.'s birthday. (See Figure 6–6.) After reading and talking about his life, I thought poetry might prove to be an interesting means of assessing the children's knowledge of the subject. Their work was varied and filled with the heart of what we'd been studying.

Nursing home residents also became the subject of poems during our first grade year:

Sam
by Caitlin Fraser-Reckard
he is sharing
and caring
that is the way
he
has
to
be

Second grade brought more sophisticated writing in all genres, and poetry was no exception. When Mia's mom came to share the history of the Day of the Dead with our class, Mia responded with this poem about the deceased children who are honored on that day. Her poem is shown in Figure 6–7. When we finished studying Harriet Tubman and the Underground Railroad, it seemed appropriate to end our study with another collection of poetry. Poetry became a natural form of self-expression for many of us and often it was the best way to say what was in our hearts and minds.

Some of the children chose to write anthologies of their own

Speeches for the World
by Jennifer Kalior

Martin Luther King, Jr.
was a good man
he fought for Civil Rights
at the time
white people and black people
couldn't do the same things
the world wasn't the
same now
Martin Luther King, Jr.
led a march to Washington, D.C.
he made
very popular speeches
for the world
you are very lucky
the world is very lucky

FIGURE 6–6   *Jennifer's poem about Martin Luther King's speech*

poetry during writing workshop. Jessie approached me one morning as I was conferring with another child. I was trying to stay focused on the child with whom I was working, but Jessie pushed her piece of paper in front of my face and asked me to read it. I looked up from that scrap of paper into the intensity of her brown eyes. I was taken aback at the depth of her poem. I asked her a couple of questions and suggested a few minor changes. This was the poem she ended up with:

FIGURE 6–7 *Mia's Day of the Dead poem*

Homeless
by Jessie Sky Wenz
as you walk by
your old heart sobs
into my young breast
you poor thing walking around
in the tough old street
your head all covered with sweat
I pick you up

> you cry on me
> but why?
> I ask you
> you tell me
> you do
> you say
> I'm on the street

It seemed that in certain situations, particularly this one with Jessie, poetry was the only way to say what needed to be said. A few words captured the essence of the children's thoughts and feelings. The poetry they wrote offered a glimpse into their hearts and at the same time left room for the reader to interpret meaning and wonder.

As second grade was nearing its end, it came time to say good-bye to Desireé, the student teacher who had been with us the entire year. Poetry seemed to be the natural vehicle for expressing our gratitude to her for all that she had brought to our class that year. The poetry the children wrote was moving. At first I thought the power came solely from their feelings for Desireé, but upon reflection I realized they were able to write as they did because we had worked hard at becoming more accomplished poets.

Music
by Jennifer Wood
Desireé's heart is full
of music that she likes to play
it is full of love too
the first time I saw you
you were beautiful
you smelled good too
you brought happiness
to the class
and happiness to the world
we love you very much
Desireé

Everything You Ever Wanted to Know. . . .

Although many of the children were engaged in creating poetic images, we had a number of writers who took up a less abstract form of writing. Several children chose to write about their particular field of

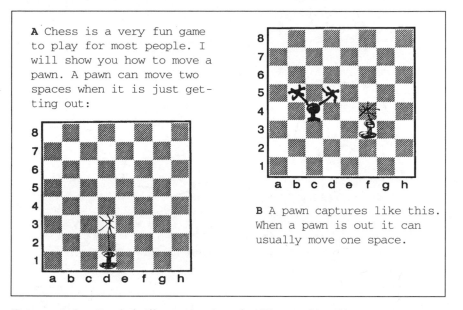

A Chess is a very fun game to play for most people. I will show you how to move a pawn. A pawn can move two spaces when it is just getting out:

B A pawn captures like this. When a pawn is out it can usually move one space.

FIGURE 6–8   *Denise's illustration from her* How to Play Chess

expertise or an area in which they were passionately interested. After reading *Howliday Inn* by James Howe, Jessica became obsessed with dachshunds. She immediately dove into research on any variety of dachshund she could find. She begged her parents for one at home, but in the end she settled for becoming the class specialist. Her book on dashchunds became a rich source of information for the rest of the class.

Emily, another dog expert with years of experience showing dogs, brought us an informative book called *How to Take Care of Dogs*. It included everything from how to check the bone structure of your new dog to what kind of food and toys should be made available. She also interjected bits of friendly advice. On the last page concerning proper food tips (in particular avoiding poisonous foods), she ended her book with: "Remember, a dead dog is a sad dog."

Denise successfully wrote a how-to book. As the sister of a nationally ranked chess player and a novice chess player herself, she outlined every detail (according to her) one needs to know to get started as a chess player in *How to Play Chess*. Through diagrams she demonstrated how to set up the pieces and make different moves. (See Figure 6–8.)

Make sure you have a lot of fun with your train and
if you don't have a lot of fun or if you have a problem with your train, call 966-4851 or 821-9732.

FIGURE 6–9   *From Ben and J. J.'s book* Hey, You Train Lovers

One of the most notable how-to books was a collaborative piece
by Ben and J. J. called *Hey, You Train Lovers.* Both passionate lovers
of model trains and all the trimmings that go along with being a train
buff, the boys wrote the book as a complete guide to model trains. It
includes such chapters as: Getting Started, Warnings, Special Scenery,

Train Jokes, and tips about joining train clubs. In their Getting Started chapter, they give this advice: "You should run your train about 40 miles an hour. If you are not satisfied, try a faster speed, but be careful that you don't run it too fast or it will run off the track." For potential train club members they offer these tips:

> Make sure you pick the right train club. Don't pick a club when you don't have a train. Don't argue or you might get thrown out. At train clubs you
>
> **1.** Show other train members your trains
> **2.** Talk about trains
> **3.** Other members show you their trains
> **4.** You go to train parks and show trains there

They end their book with a final statement. (See Figure 6–9.)

Charlie was another child who wrote about his obsession (Glover, 1992). His passion was professional sports, especially the Phoenix Suns and the National Basketball Association (NBA). Charlie wrote extensively about the National Football League (NFL) and the NBA and became the school expert on sports. Other children would seek him out when then needed pertinent information. Several of his published works, including his final book *The Suns' Book of 1990*, dealt with the successes and failures of professional sports. (See Figure 6–10.)

During class studies children would pick an area of specialization and write a summary of their findings. For example, when we studied Japan each child picked an aspect of Japanese culture to research and report back to the class. While our animal study was going on, Jessie decided to research the relationship between two of her favorite animals. One day in the planning stages of her research she commented, "I'll look in books, check things out. I've always been interested in this, and if I work really hard, I think I can learn a lot." Most of the children approached research with this same enthusiasm, and we were well informed on such topics as Japanese houses, white tigers, the respiratory system, and forest animals. It didn't really matter *what* the children were studying and writing about as much as *how* they went about learning the process. As they worked, they came to see the value of writing as a means of communicating knowledge to the rest of the world. By sharing what they knew through writing, the

A With L.A. in game one the Suns pushed the tempo up but late in the game the Suns were down 101-98. But then Kevin Johnson made a three point basket then they took the lead 104-101. Then Magic Johnson made the first and missed the second on purpose and K. J. came up with the ball. Two, one, aaaaaaaa . . . the Suns won 104-102.

B Tom Chambers finished up as the fourth player to score 13,020 points in the NBA. K. J. had a record setting of 9,000 points and 10.5 assists for each game. The Suns were the most scoring team in the NBA.

FIGURE 6–10 *Charlie's illustrations from his book* The Sun's Book of 1990

children not only gained a greater sense of self-worth but truly contributed to the educational process of others in their lives.

The Seed News

As the children gathered information for research reports, they learned about another mechanism for gathering and reporting information: the school newspaper. The second-grade tradition of producing *The Seed News* was established during the year the children were in first grade. They practiced their skills as journalists that year by submitting several pieces ranging from poetry to J. J.'s report of a chemi-

> ```
> The Excitement of P.E.
> by Tara Waymire and Maureen Scholl
>
> P.E. is fun because it teaches us to
> be a P.E. teacher. We play lots of
> games like Animal Keepers and Spuds.
> We play Jail and we play catch. We
> line up on the line. And we try to get
> the tail off the donkey. We play Cow-
> boys and Indians and Horses. We play
> Johnny Cross. The P.E. teacher's name
> is Bobbie. She has weird sunglasses.
> We hug her. We think she is nice. We
> make her happy. She does nice things.
> We think the teacher is nice. When we
> come inside we always say,
>
>              "We love P.E.!"
> ```

FIGURE 6–11   *A* Seed News *article on the school's P.E. teacher*

cal fire across the street from the school. Some of the children did feature articles about favorite staff members and their contributions to the school community. (See Figure 6–11.) Others wanted to share the recipe from a pie baking experience. (See Figure 6–12.)

When we all graduated to second grade, we inherited the newspaper's production. We gave the paper its current name (it was previously called *The Awakening Seed Republic*) and organized regular sections we wanted to include. Naturally we had a large poetry section, in addition to: Sports, Class News, Staff, How-to Hints, Pets, Special Interest Stories, Book Reviews, and Recipes. Each issue included feature articles. (See Figure 6–13.)

The children learned to interview people so they could write a feature story about them. (See Figure 6–14.) They learned to ask questions that would make their subject tell them a story. And they learned how to summarize information rather than writing down everything that was said in the interview, including their own questions:

Writing book reviews also presented new challenges for writers.

Pies
by Katie Sanchez and Jennifer Kalior

<u>Recipe for Pies:</u>
10 spoonfuls of flour
1 pinch of salt
4 spoonfuls of oil
4 spoonfuls of water

After that you stir it up really good.
Then you put in the apples. Cut them up.
Then you make the two crusts. Put them on
and then you put it in the oven. And then
cook it for a little while. You take it
out of the oven. The pie is delicious.

FIGURE 6–12 *Katie and Jennifer's article for* The Seed News.

Charlie was one of the more successful reviewers because he not only shared information about the book but also kept his voice in his writing. (See Figure 6–15.)

A number of the articles ended up being written collaboratively.

THE SEED NEWS

© 1989 Awakening Seed Press

October 1989   **1130 W. 23rd Street • Tempe, Arizona 85282**   **$1.00**

7th Annual Seed Halloween Carnival

by Jessica Rodd

The Halloween Carnival is Friday, October 27th. We dress up in our costumes and come to the school at night. This year we are going to have a new thing. It's called the Dungeon of Doom. If you want to put someone in jail you pay a ticket. To get out you pay a ticket. We also do things like the Haunted House. There is a lion who grabs your leg and a mummy that keeps on saying, "Come to me, come to me." There's a turtle race with cardboard turtles. Five can play. There's also food and you can win prizes too. We usually have a play.

David Greenberg Visits the Seed
by Elizabeth Hobson

David Greenberg is a good author. He writes very funny books. He makes his home in Portland, Oregon. He did his first book named <u>Slugs</u> when he was twenty years old. It got published when he was twenty-five years old.

FIGURE 6–13   *Front page of* The Seed News.

Noah and Jenny were one of the more effective teams with their feature article on Dr. Martin Luther King, Jr. (See Figure 6–16.) They sat side by side for several writing periods, deciding who should write which parts of his life and then how to order those parts. Jenny would write for awhile, and Noah would tell her what to put on the paper.

71

STAFF

THE DEBRA STORIES: An Interview with Debra Kalior
by Jennifer Kalior

Even though I'm seven, I'm old enough I can interview my mom. I struggled to get her to sit down from her duty. She sat down. "Finally," I said in a shivery voice. I asked her some questions and she answered in the greatest way possible.

"I enjoy working with kids and I feel like making a special science center for the kids." I asked her some questions about her classroom. She said, "I try to think of things that they like and I make it into the science center." In my own words I think that's what she was trying to tell me. She said, "My favorite things to do with the kids are... dun-da-dun... the science center."

Like a lawyer in court I said, "Why did you decide to be a teacher instead of being an engineer?" She said, "I like working with people and I feel that children have lots of important things to teach me!" I set my paper down with one hundred answers and I started writing this report.

An Interview of Mary Glover
by Jessica Rodd and Caitlin Fraser-Reckard

Mary is 38 years old and she likes to play racquetball. Her favorite color is turquoise. She says her favorite poet is Nikki Giovanni. Her favorite plant is the red rose. She likes teaching because it is exciting and it is a fun way to make the world a better place. Her phone number is 894-1143. She likes classical music because it is very uplifting. Her favorite characters in a book are probably the Stupids. Her favorite opera is "Where the Wild Things Are."

DESIRÉE
by Jessica Spencer

Desirée is our student teacher. She likes teaching here because she likes being part of a school that is an excellent education. She picked this school because Mary came to her class at ASU and she agreed with what Mary was saying about educating children. So she asked Mary about working with her.

Desiree is from Seattle, Washington. She likes the weather here but she doesn't like the summers and she misses the lakes and oceans. She came to Arizona because she and her husband needed a change. She wanted to be a teacher because she likes children and she likes to help them learn. Her hobby is playing the piano.

STEVE
by Jacob Dayley

Steve is a person who likes kids. He likes to be with young people. He is a good teacher at this school. Steve believes the kids can learn if he gives them the chance. Steve helps with the P.E. program with his partner Peter. Steve likes kids so much because they are like a flower ready to blossom and he likes to watch that happen.

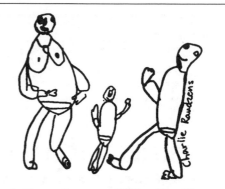

<u>Freedom Train</u>
by Dorothy Sterling
reviewed by Charlie Raudzens

I would like to do a book review on <u>Freedom Train</u>. It is a book about a girl that grows up and lives in the South and escapes to the North. She comes to Niagara Falls and comes back to the South and goes to the border of Canada. Why she keeps going back and forth is because she didn't want to know that she was free and other black people weren't. It is a wonderful story. So for that book report this is Charlie Raudzens signing out for the book report.

Anthony Browne--<u>Willy the Wimp</u>
by Charlie Raudzens

I read the book <u>Willy the Wimp</u>. There are 17 pages in the book. It is a very, very funny book. My favorite part is when Willy joins a body building club. <u>Willy the Wimp</u> is a great book for the whole family. So far it is Charlie Raudzens' favorite book.

FIGURE 6–15   The Seed News *book reviews*

Then he would take over as scribe, and Jenny would scan the dictionary for the words they didn't know how to spell. There were a few days when they'd call me over for clarification of some point, such as what passive resistance really meant and how that related to Rosa Parks on the bus. Satisfied with my explanation, they sent me away and returned to their piece. For Noah and Jenny, as well as their other classmates, working this way served a variety of purposes. It helped them learn to negotiate with another person. Decisions had to be made cooperatively, teaching them to be more receptive and toler-

THE SEED NEWS
© 1990 Awakening Seed Press

February 1990   1130 W. 23rd Street • Tempe, Arizona 85282 $1.00

Celebration of Peace

In Honor of Dr. Martin Luther King, Jr.'s Birthday

by Noah Underwood and Jennifer Wood

Martin Luther King wanted peace. He won a Nobel Peace Prize. He led many marches. Martin Luther King read about Gandhi. Martin Luther King was a great leader and a fighter. But he didn't fight with a gun or a knife, but with words.

Martin Luther King never met with Gandhi. Also Gandhi wanted peace too. The KKK burned crosses in people's yards but Martin Luther King wanted to stop it. If a black man got on a bus and a white man came and the bus was full, they would tell the black man to get off the bus. Martin Luther King heard about Thoreau's idea of passive resistance. Passive resistance meant that people would walk instead of riding on the bus. Martin Luther King was assassinated in 1968 on a balcony by a gun.

Martin Luther King was minister. He was a black man. His family still gives speeches about Martin Luther King.

FIGURE 6–16   *Noah and Jenny's article for Dr. King's birthday*

ant of other people's ideas. And it enabled all of the children to see that working together often produces results that are superior, and certainly more surprising, than those created individually.

Working on *The Seed News* made our entire circle of journalists more acutely aware of the audience beyond our classroom. We also learned about audience in yet another type of writing—letters.

Letters

Letter writing was practiced in three ways in our classroom. One was the dialogue journal kept between each child and myself. In writing twice a week, the journal became a series of letters exchanged between us. The content of these letters varied. Many of the children were able to develop their voice in their journal writing. Often the journal entries contained humor and focused on the daily business of our personal lives. The page from Jacob's journal in Figure 6–17 is typical.

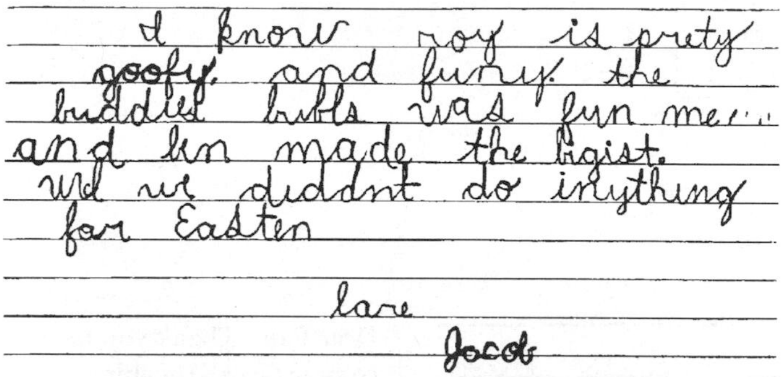

> *I know* roy *is* prety
> goofy. and funy *the*
> buddies buble *was* fun me...
> and ben *made the* bigist.
> *we* we diddnt *do* inything
> for Easten
>
>   lave
>   Jacob

**I know Roy [from the nursing home] is pretty
goofy and funny. The buddies bubbles was fun.
Me and Ben made the biggest. And we didn't do
anything for Easter.**

Love, Jacob

FIGURE 6–17   *Jacob's journal*

The dialogue journal served several purposes. It enabled me to know my students in a personal and private way through writing. The journal became a record of the growth of our friendship over time. And it offered a channel for both the children and myself to share thoughts or feelings that were more difficult to say in person.

Other logs were kept for science, literature study, and the nursing home visits. These were different from the dialogue journals in that I did not respond to the children each time in writing. In a sense, all these logs were more like "letters to myself." In other words, each child would record thoughts, feelings, and responses to experiences as a sort of reminder of the moment. The writing slowed down the thinking process and allowed time for reflection. Although the children knew I would read what they had written, the audience was primarily themselves. These logs served as a documentation of learning and historical events.

A third letter writing activity was corresponding with pen pals and people outside of our immediate circle. We wrote letters to get information from people far away, letters to former classmates, and letters to friends we knew only through writing. We had pen pals at a nearby school and pen pals in Maine. These letters kept us in touch

Dear Pam TacyoU Four
CaMiNG I Lice ToHiNG
iT. WaR DiD You GOt iT?
MaB ScM DY You COD
come TO MY HOWS. aND
BRING THe SKLTIN To LoVe BeN

Dear Pam, Thank you for coming. I like touching it. Where did you get it? Maybe some day you could come to my house. And bring the skeleton too. Love, Ben

FIGURE 6–18 *Ben's thank-you note*

with the world outside of our circle in a very personal way. We also wrote letters to people who came to our class to share their expertise. When Pam brought her human skeleton during first grade, she received a thick envelope full of thanks. Sometimes these letters were written as a group on large chart paper and at other times they were written individually as Ben did in Figure 6–18. Writing letters reminded us that we are social beings and need communications with others to keep our lives rich and interesting. As time passed it became evident that it was the social nature of living and learning that kept our classroom alive.

Oh, No!   7

❧ The room is a complete mess. Small groups of children are stationed in every available space. Large pieces of mat board, which are strewn all over the tables and floor, serve as the bases for the three-dimensional games the children are creating. Tape, scraps of paper, scissors, and other necessary items litter the space not taken up by bodies or mat board. There is an abundance of talk and excitement. Ben, Noah, and J. J. are in the process of designing a game called *Spies: A Special Game*. Their game is an intricate series of tests and traps players encounter as they travel along the path of the game board. There are tiny swords and jewel boxes to be found. Dangers include a falling bridge, falling trees and boulders, and a volcano. There is constant negotiation and renegotiation going on among the game's creators. As I approach them they offer this explanation:

> You try to get to the orb of Karnos. If you get a sword you can go past the teepee, but then you have to put it away because it wouldn't be fair. You could pass the game easily so it can only be used once. You have to put your sword in a jewel box. We're going to make jewel boxes for however many people are going to play. You can get little tiny jewels too.

A while later I ask how they get their ideas. Noah says, "They just come to us." Ben adds, "We wait until somebody says, 'Hey, I've got a good idea!' Then we use it. But it depends on if we like the idea." They slip into further discussion about the sword. There is talk about whether it's a sword or a dagger. J. J. says he is making a pair of special shoes to put over in the magic room. Their focus is again on the game, and I slip away to check in on another group.

The process of making games was but one example of the social nature of our class. Days were filled with talk as we shared our thoughts and ideas. Everything we did was social, beginning each day with our circle. The socializing continued during lunch time as children told each other stories of wild escapades. At the end of the day, when chairs needed to be stacked up and all pencils had to be returned to their appropriate containers, the intricate web of social interaction was still being woven. Pairs of children chattered away as they discovered the best way to wash out paint brushes or make decisions about which newspapers could be folded up and reused the next day. They talked through their plans for what they would do during their lunch recess or how they might spend free time. Talk and stories shared in a social way contributed to the level of involvement experienced by each person in the classroom. The stories enabled us to know each other more deeply, strengthening the ties between us. We realized that we had all come together to learn, and we needed each other to get better at it. Maxine Greene (1978) writes:

> We all learn to become human, as is well known, within a community of some kind or by means of a social medium. The more fully engaged we are, the more we can look through others' eyes, the more richly individual we become. The activities that compose learning not only engage us in our own quests for answers and for meanings; they also serve to initiate us into the communities of scholarship and (if our perspectives widen sufficiently) into the human community, in its largest and richest sense. (p. 3)

The way we read, the way we thought, and the way we talked about the world was all a part of that initiation into the human community. How we connected to each other and, in turn, to life as it flowed in and out of our classroom, was profoundly affected by the social climate in which we lived. The social aspect of our class was valued, and it was difficult to find a separation between the talk of work and the talk of play. In fact, I doubt that any of us ever made much of a separation between the two—we were all so deeply engrossed in our daily living together that work and play took on the same quality.

The three previous chapters have focused on how we worked and learned together to study topics of interest, experience literature and become a community of writers. In this chapter I'd like to examine how that same sense of camaraderie extended into activities that were more play oriented.

My thinking about play evolved during the two years I spent with these children. I was able to see the playfulness in the way they worked together and at the same time the seriousness of their play.

Playing with pattern blocks to create intricate symmetrical patterns, a fun and exciting process, was hard work. Working together on a mural of *Abel's Island* took intense concentration, but the colors and textures were mixed in a way that brought joy and delight to the artist as well as the viewer. The play aspect of our classroom was alive and well in several frequently occurring events. These events generally fell into four categories: projects, games, free choice, and lunch.

Projects

Projects were a part of everything we did. Most of our content studies included them in some way. When we had parties, the children organized themselves into teams to make chains of colored paper and then figured out how to hang them up with minimal assistance. They worked for weeks on puppets and scripts for the shows they wanted to perform before a live audience. Our Japanese festival was a celebration of projects. One Halloween project in first grade was particularly memorable. It contained the best of work and play.

It is mid-October. The mat board pile and paper towel tubes are overflowing on the art shelf, in desperate need of consumption. Our room still has that beginning-of-the-year look. I think a few Halloween decorations would improve the aesthetics of our environment. Knowing the benefits of having children work in teams, I concoct the idea of having small groups (4 to 5 students) construct haunted houses. In addition to decorating the room and using up the extra art materials, the project will also help children learn to work collaboratively and practice their communication skills.

Several days are devoted to the haunted houses. They surpass anything I could have ever imagined. Jennifer invents an ingenious idea for making miniature framed portraits for her group's house by drawing with markers and then gluing them to the inside of a clear plastic lid. When the glue dries and the picture shows through it takes on an eery, slightly altered look. Jessie's group designs a unique series of lamps for their house, and Ben's group is successful at constructing moving floorboards. At one point during their demonstration Ben exclaims, "See, Mary, when they walk on these floors they'll go c-r-e-a-k!" He has figured out a way to make the mat board curl up so it resembled warped wooden floorboards. Their house not only has movable floorboards but also includes other elaborate structures filled with traps, hidden creatures, and mysterious sights and sounds. Maureen's group uses their ingenuity by enlisting the assistance of Cathy, a visiting engineer friend to help them secure the walls of their haunted house. Two rolls of clear packing tape and a lot of talk later, they have the most stable walls in town. When the houses are slathered with thick coats of black paint and accented with a rainbow assortment of other colors, they seem to take on a life of their own. The only thing that matches the final visual product is the rich, descriptive language produced in the process.

Through this process the children learned to negotiate ideas and respect the possibilities others offered. It was a delightful experience for everyone, as were the end results. The work was good because it was infused with playfulness.

Games

Midway through second grade I became interested in games. The work of Constance Kamii (1989) introduced me to the idea of using games to promote children's autonomy in both their thinking and their actions. We used many of her suggested games for mathematics with great success. I wanted to take the game concept further and have the children invent their own. Once initiated, games took over as one of the favorite pastimes for the remainder of second grade.

Of course games were being created continually during free time, on the playground, and throughout the school day whenever the imagination had an opportunity to be exercised. The games that fascinated me the most, however, were the board games that the children designed in the classroom.

Four of the boys are sprawled on the floor. They hover over Ben's latest brainchild, a board game called *Oh, No!* It has a similar format to the game Candyland with a few added twists. Each player begins the game having just been in a plane crash and starts by saying, "Oh, no!" The game proceeds with each child rolling two dice. The two numbers are added or subtracted from each other, depending on the symbol that appears on yet another die. Brian has just determined the correct answer to the mathematical problem, and he wins the privilege of rolling one last die to see how many spaces he is allowed to move. Along the way there are, naturally, numerous traps and pitfalls to keep each player from reaching his or her destination. The game is governed by the set of rules written out in Figure 7–1.

Oh, No! set off an avalanche of board game mania. Soon our

Oh, No! Game Rules

If player lands on a[n] "Oh No" they have to go around it until they can continue their journey. The other ones should be written down. If a player lands on top of you you have to go back to START.

FIGURE 7–1   *From Ben's* Oh, No! *game*

class had a collection of board games that would give Milton-Bradley a run for the money. There was *Under the Sea*, an adventure game with shark-infested waters and other dangers encountered under the oceans, and *The White Tigers*, a jungle game about the endangered species of the same name. *Slavery* was the title of a game about slaves escaping from their masters and vicious dogs, via the Underground Railroad. (See Figure 7–2.) If they made it safely past all the dangers they would arrive in Canada, finally free. *Oh, No!* also had an offspring: *Jungle Oh, No!*

The board games soon evolved into three-dimensional games. These games took over our classroom and for a week left no space for anything else until the games were finally taken home. Had I not insisted the children take the games home, I doubt that we would have accomplished much else for the remainder of the year. The games not only consumed our classroom living space but took everyone's attention away from anything else.

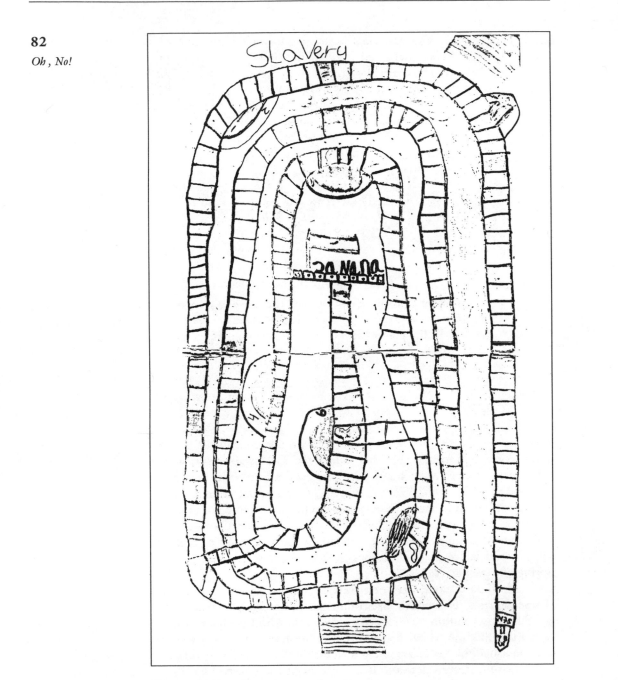

FIGURE 7–2   Slavery *game board*

Before the games were taken home, we had a sharing celebration. In the end Ben, Noah, and J. J.'s game *Spies: A Special Game* became an elaborate maze of falling trees, control buttons (much like the Wizard's set-up in *The Wizard of Oz*) for setting off various traps, water canals, and those intricate little swords stored in their special jewel boxes. Another game created by Mia and Jennifer was called *Finders Keepers*. It was a series of challenges each player had to meet in order to obtain various treasures, such as a queen's crown, a necklace, and a container of jewels.

Most of the games, with the exception of *Oh, No!* and *Under the Sea*, never developed to the point where they were played repeatedly with a consistent set of rules. The rules, and the game boards themselves, continually changed. The children's priority with the games was the social aspect of their creation. The final product was secondary to the joyful process of inventing the games in the first place.

Free Choice

Jessica has organized herself at a table with her writing folder and a collection of Laura Ingalls Wilder books. During her free choice time, she has chosen to write what she calls a book report, which includes "a little about each book, then a little about Laura Ingalls Wilder's life." Nearby several of the other girls are trying out the new, very popular smelly markers. Jennifer has just made a bookmark that has a tiny book attached to it. She shows it to me and says, "See, I've even put about the author!" Noah and Maureen are over in the area of the room where science materials are stored. Recent experiments with electrical equipment have drawn their attention to a box of discarded wires. They take on the challenge of trying to remove the plastic coating from the ends of the wire so they can continue with their experiments. Some of the wires are more cooperative than others. A particularly stubborn one is tied to the chart rack and pulled on with a pair of pliers. Noah eventually succeeds in removing the plastic. Maureen is pleased with him and says, "Noah's cool. Noah's tough. Noah's a dude!" Noah gets embarrassed and walks over to where Charlie is sitting, engrossed in making signs for Georgia Tech's game in the NCAA Final Four. He decides to join him and begins to draw a Teenage Mutant Ninja Turtle. In another corner of the room a lively game of *Oh, No!* is going on. Every child is busy with some sort of personally selected activity. It is free choice time, everyone's favorite and happiest part of the day.

Free choice was a time we all valued and a segment of the day in which some of the most valuable learning transpired. Free choice was strictly a social time, although children would frequently choose work from earlier in the day to pursue. For example, during first grade some of the children who had shown an interest were introduced to cursive writing. Others became fascinated with it and asked to do the same during free choice. Before long several children were madly writing away in cursive, talking nonstop as they went along. I couldn't have planned a more lively social event!

Children seldom worked alone during free choice. It was a time where socializing was at its best. A pack of them would choose to play dress-ups, often concocting complicated scenarios together. Their imaginative play was filled with talk and social exchanges. The board games were popular during free choice, which brought forth animated conversations and negotiations. Some children consistently chose the same activity at free choice time. Charlie could almost always be found with a friend drawing pictures of basketball players. It was a time when many children worked on independent projects. For example, Maureen and Elizabeth spent several free choice hours making book markers to sell to earn money for Elizabeth's Quaker meeting. Regardless of the activity, it was always a good time to observe the social dynamics of the class. It was a time to just *be* with the children without having to be concerned with teaching. It was truly a time for learning, and I was always impressed with how concentrated the children were during this part of our day. They took this time for play and independent work seriously. I saw very little time being wasted during free choice. It was a time for strengthening the social bonds between classmates as well as giving children the opportunity to choose their own learning activities.

Although it was not a part of our regular free choice time, there was an additional time with some of the children that carried the same tone as free choice. We called it "Art Day." What it amounted to was a few of the children hanging around the room after school for an hour or so mostly doing art. It was a casual and relaxing time, always optional and voluntary. We would talk and paint or work on the crayon melting trays. Jennifer was one of the regulars for Art Day. She enjoyed working collaboratively with others to make colorfully designed paper with crayons and watercolor, which would later be cut and glued to make greeting cards as a fundraiser for the school's scholarship fund. On other occasions she would spend intense periods of time drawing highly fashionable characters with markers and pens.

It was always a spontaneous time where the energy of the day slowed down, and we could relax into pleasant conversation.

A regular component of Art Day was cleaning the room. Some of the children liked this activity as much as the art itself. Maureen was a whiz with a sponge and a spray bottle. She could clean those tables until they were sanitized enough to eat off them (not that I'd ever think of trying it!). The cleaning gave children an excuse to hang around and be together in our room without the usual level of activity. It was a time for giving individual attention and for being social in a completely relaxed way. Art Day was always spontaneous and never planned ahead of time. It was always fun.

Lunch

Our school is small. There is no central cafeteria, so the children bring their lunches and eat them in the classroom. Generally the process takes a half hour each day before they go outside for recess. On most days I chose to eat with them. Lunch was not a particularly relaxing time. It was boisterous with socialization at its peak. Lunch, and the recess period following it, seemed to test the strength of the social ties that held us together. Relationships were formed and dissolved as plans for outside activities were put in order. Arguments might crop up if someone shared their Fun Fruits with one friend and not another. At least one disturbance per day could be counted on with one child's box of apple juice getting squeezed and squirted all over the table by another child. We worked at manners, succeeding at using them some days more than others. Sport challenges were made; markers and paper were gathered for drawing activities; and friends who needed to stick together found each other. It was a time, more than any other in the day, when girls and boys separated into their own camps. Occasionally a brave girl or boy would cross the line and join up with members of the opposite gender. As much as I tried to promote intermingling of girls and boys in classroom activities, this separation took place. It occurred for several reasons.

The primary reason was simply a matter of interest. Boys and girls just had different things to talk about. The boys often fooled around at lunch, to the point where spills and messes would occur. There was hardly a day when someone didn't have to be reminded to pick up food off the floor, dropped or thrown there in the midst of some outrageous story. The girls tended to eat in smaller groups, sometimes telling secrets about each other or the boys. A common topic was who loved who that day and how they were going to be involved in "chase and kiss" games at recess. It seemed to be an age where interest in the opposite sex was beginning to bud and lunch time stirred up these inclinations. Interests seemed to fluctuate between really liking each other and wanting to do almost anything possible to be annoying or disgusting. It was a time of testing the waters for future relationships.

Another reason for the separation had to do with numbers. Since there were only 6 boys and 12 girls, the boys used lunch as a time for gathering their resources. The boys held their own but seemed to need this time to regroup in order to take on all the female energy in the class. Jacob was an exception. He was the one boy who managed to take on most of the girls at recess (and other times of the day) in a game called "Kitty." Jacob was the kitty, and several of the girls would pretend to be his caretakers. This game was ongoing, and he seemed to like the game as much as the girls. On a good day most of the class got into it.

Along with the obvious food and talk that contributed to the social life in our class, there was clean-up. After lunch there were assigned jobs for a few children to do: wiping the tables and sweeping floors. These jobs rotated weekly so everyone had a turn. Some of the children loved these duties and would spend a long time spraying the tables, then meticulously wiping them off with paper towels in order to avoid going out to recess. Still others cleaned with a frenzy, often not doing a very thorough job, just so they could get outside to play basketball. The cleaning, like the eating, had its social aspects as well. It was an opportunity for children to practice working as a team, negotiating how a certain task should be accomplished. They could feel like they were contributing to the community by being helpful. Cleaning up after everyone else also served as a reminder to pay more attention to personal messes made while eating. The same child who could care less about leaving wrappers and smashed chips on the floor one week might be disgusted with his or her peers the following week commenting, "Those kids are disgusting!" It was good practice for putting the Golden Rule into action.

In addition to all of the rich social interaction that went on at lunch, it was also the time of day when most of the conflicts arose. While in the classroom, the organization of the day and the way we worked usually kept everyone productively engaged with a minimum of difficulties. But when that structure was removed and children were left to themselves to organize their play and other social arrangements, problems did arise. The problem of sharing or not sharing equipment, such as jump ropes brought from home, was a perennial problem. A child might permit one friend to use her jump rope and exclude another. I would frequently be greeted with these conflicts when the children returned to the room after lunch recess. The situation was complicated for me in that I wasn't present when the problem occurred so I had to rely on information given by other teachers or the children. My first comment was usually, "Tell me what happened." Each child involved would be given the opportunity to tell his or her version of the story, and often I would solicit information from a third or fourth party. In most cases the problem was not an isolated event, and I tried to help the children see how their actions contributed to the trouble. I'd then ask, "How could this situation be prevented in the future? What can we all learn from this?" I found that by getting them involved in solving the problem, the problems were less likely to recur. After all children had a chance to say what they needed to say, I would usually end the discussion by reminding them that we all needed to work together to see that school remained a safe and happy place for everyone.

Although this was one of the most challenging aspects of the class, it was also one of the most important. Kohlberg and Lickona (1987) suggest that healthy conflict helps children develop moral judgment and entertain the perspective of others, particularly those who are in disagreement. Working through conflicts helped individual children to grow—to become more patient and fair with their peers. As a group, learning to solve these problems tended to strengthen the bonds that tied us together. Knowing that certain actions would lead to hurt feelings enabled everyone be more aware of how to treat each other. And going through the process of establishing guidelines to make our classroom a safe and happy place for everyone helped each child to feel that his or her contribution to the whole was important. By participating in this conflict resolving ritual each person's commitment to the class, and their sense of caring, became stronger. It was the level of caring that, at the end of the school year, made it so hard to let go.

8 Then They Were Gone

A perplexing phenomenon occurred in our classroom during the last few weeks of school. The children began arguing constantly over petty issues. The air was thick with tension. It appeared that our harmonious community was falling apart. I brought up my concerns at a staff meeting, and my colleagues helped me to see that there was an underlying grieving process going on that needed to be brought to the surface. We were all anticipating the end of the school year, but nobody was talking about it.

The next morning we sat together in our opening circle, and I told them I was having some sad feelings about the year coming to an end. I said it was really hard for me to think of not being with them anymore after all the time we had spent together. I said, "I thought some of you might be feeling the same way." Tears quickly followed these words, opening up a floodgate of responses from the children. Some cried, some expressed how scared they were to go to a new school, and still others sat there very quietly, saying with their eyes and faces what they couldn't say with their mouths. After a rather lengthy discussion about change and transitions we all felt better. When we were finished we hugged each other, laughed uproariously, and then moved on with our day. Although the air was cleared somewhat by this discussion, bringing the year to an end was not easy for any of us. We tried to stay cheerful, but the letting go was hard, especially for me.

After our discussion I realized the importance of bringing to a close the classroom life we had shared. The process of ending the year, I learned, is as vital to a classroom community as all the work we do at the beginning of the year to establish that community. I realized too that as teachers it is necessary for us to lead the way. Along with the children, I came to know that the delicate process of dispersing a circle of friends is a time for closing a door. A chapter of history in our lives has been written, and there comes a point where it must end. But in that moment of closing a door, there is an equally wonderful opportunity for another one to open. I had to remind myself and the children of this fact. I had to help them remember that these times of letting go in our lives needn't only be sad and that actually they can also be times of hope—for it is in these moments of opening doors that the future calls us forward.

In the midst of our closure conversation, Bill walked into our room and noticed the sad faces and empty tissue boxes. One of the children said something about wanting me to be their teacher forever. He said, "You know, if you had Mary for the rest of your school life, all of those other teachers would miss out on the experience of having you for their students. Now that wouldn't be fair, would it?" The children thought about it and decided that it probably wouldn't be fair. In that moment, I think we all began to realize that it was time for us to take what we had known together and share it with the rest of the world. If we remained in our same classroom indefinitely, we would not only prevent others from sharing experiences with us but we would also miss out on the surprises that lay around the corner for each of us. If we stayed together, we would be just like the Tuck family in *Tuck Everlasting*, stuck at the moment in time when they drank the waters of life everlasting. As time moved on the Tucks were unhappy with their life because it never changed—and we would be too. Life was calling us ahead to the future and it was time for our experience together to come to completion.

In Honor of Great Performances

Closure occurred in a number of ways for our class, both as a group and as individuals. During the last two weeks of school, we went around the circle and made a list on chart paper of books that needed to be published before school's end. When a book was finished, its author placed a bright orange sticker by his or her name to indicate that the publication process was completed. As each book reached publication, its author sat in the author's chair and shared it with the class. At the year's end the books went home to be shared with families and friends.

When it was time for Desireé to leave us at the end of her student teaching, we secretly made her a book of poetry and self-portraits. Children brought an array of food and other gifts that were given to her at the surprise party we had planned in her honor. We presented the book to her at that time as well, in celebration of the extraordinary months we had shared with her.

In addition to the surprise book for Desireé, there were other secrets in the works. These were unveiled on the last regular day of school, our Awards Day. Over the years it has become a tradition to give each child in our school an award for outstanding achievement in

FIGURE 8–1 *Jennifer's award*

some area of his or her school life. The awards are all individualized
and cover a range of possibilities. Sometimes funny and at other times
more serious, they are given to celebrate an outstanding performance
or effort by each child. This year's awards were no exception.

Mounted on the recycled paper we had made on Earth Day,
each award was given along with a short speech about each child. Jennifer was honored for her collaborative writing work with Tara. (See
Figure 8–1.) The two of them had worked long and hard on a piece
of fiction together. They weren't getting along very well, and their

FIGURE 8–2 *Noah's plate*

occasional conflicts brought many tears as they went through the process of trying to decide how to use each other's ideas. It was nothing short of a miracle that they completed the book and remained friends. When asked later why they stuck it out until the end they said, "It was better to be disgusted with the person you're with than staring at a blank piece of paper." It seemed appropriate that they should be awarded for this job well done.

Jacob received the Math Whiz Kid Award for being able to do just about anything with numbers. He was a child who could turn any life situation into a math problem! Jessie was given the Bionic Buddy Award for outstanding buddy reading beyond the call of duty. She'd had a particularly trying year with her very active buddy reader and acknowledgement for this effort on her part seemed appropriate. Brian, who was always a good sport on and off the court, earned the Happy Hoopster Award for his exceptional sportsmanlike conduct. And Ben, who could have received a variety of awards for being exceptional in one way or another, was fittingly presented the Oh, No! Award for his innovative designing of board games. The irony of Ben's award was that he had to struggle to the front of the room on crutches to receive it. He had recently broken his foot by falling backwards into an empty swimming pool.

In addition to the children's awards, I gave them each a copy of the poem I had written about our class (appears in the front of the book). I had fully intended to read it to them, but in the end was unable to do so. There were too many memories flooding through my heart and mind. When I had finished handing out all of the children's awards, it was their turn to do the giving.

Earlier in the semester, while I was away at a conference, one of the parents and Desireé had organized the plate project. Each child drew a brightly colored design on a circular piece of paper that was sent through the mail to a company that transfers the designs onto a plate. On Awards Day, Jennifer stepped forward first and handed me a plate. She also tearfully read me a poem. Initially I thought she was presenting the gift to me on behalf of the entire class. I was soon to discover that *each* child had made a plate for me. (See Figure 8–2.) And each had written a poem.

Go Back Into Your Mind
by Jessie Wenz
For the year is over
and I am leaving
and when you think of me
you don't have to think
and go in the back of your mind
Just look around
See what is mine
What I did
I'm growing up
But think of what I did
when I was little
I love you

In offering the gift of a plate and a poem, each child had unknowingly presented two symbols of what we had become: a circle of learners who cared deeply for each other and who also took the time to express those feelings through writing and other forms of communication.

Responsible, Forever

After gifts were exchanged and final hugs were given, we said our good-byes. Some of the children were staying on for the summer program, a series of mini-courses during June and July where children in mixed-age groups concentrate on specific subject matter such as botany, mask making, sewing, dramatic production, or scientific experimentation. For the students remaining, the good-byes were delayed until June or July when they finally departed from the school. But for our class, it was the last time we would ever stand together as a whole.

Thinking back on this time, I am reminded of *The Little Prince*, one of my favorite childhood stories. In the book the little prince meets a fox and they strike up a friendship. The fox explains to the little prince that in order to be real friends one must establish ties or become "tamed." As their relationship evolves they tell each other many secrets, and the little prince tells the fox of another friend on a faraway planet, his rose.

When their hour of departure arrives, the fox begins to cry because the prince is leaving him. Misunderstanding his tears, the little prince thinks he has done no good by taming the fox. The fox responds with a few words of advice:

> And now here is my secret, a very simple secret: It is only with the heart that one can see rightly; what is essential is invisible to the eye. . . . It is the time you have wasted for your rose that makes your rose so important. . . . You become responsible, forever, for what you have tamed.
> (p. 70)

Each one of us had become friends with one another. We were tamed by the ties we had established. Regardless of the separate paths down which life would take us, we would always share a responsibility to each other because of the time we had spent together.

As Jessie once said in a literary discussion, "It's like we're adding on to an old story to make a new one." All a part of the ongoing story of teachers and children, our two-year class had composed its own new story. In time our story would be the old one, added on to by other students and teachers in new circles of friends

One morning the boy named Bill woke up. He started to
stretch. He looked around. He saw two big Tookies. He
was startled. He couldn't believe his eyes. He called
his cat, Herbie the talking cat. Herbie could not believe his cat eyes either.

FIGURE 8–3 *From Noah's sequel* Tookies on Earth

who learn together. Our responsibility lies in always honoring that
story, remembering it and keeping it close to our hearts. And, when
the time is right, we are also responsible for telling our story to others
who care to hear it.

One Last Story

About a year after Noah published *The Planet Tookie*, he wrote its sequel, *Tookies on Earth*. The Tookies suddenly appear one morning at

FIGURE 8–4   *Bill, the cat, and the Tookies ready for an adventure*

the bedside of "the boy named Bill." Bill is startled to see them, as is Herbie, his talking cat. (See Figure 8–3.) He asks them why they are here, and they say it is because they missed him. The boy named Bill finds disguises for them, and they go off to have an adventuresome day together. (See Figure 8–4.)

The boy named Bill teaches the Tookies how to skateboard, and Bill examines the Tookies' rocketship in his backyard. Herbie introduces the Tookies to Fig Newtons, which they love. Then they go bowling and check out the local video arcade. Before long it is time for the Tookies to return home. (See Figure 8–5.)

I realized, after reading Noah's story, that it was a metaphor for my experience with these children and their experience with me. We'd created our history together—two years worth, as a matter of fact—but like the Tookies, after a second visitation, it was time for all of us to move on to other people and experiences. We would take with us the memories of those moments shared as we traveled off to other times and spaces. The bonds of love we established with one another would surpass time and distance, held intact by the memories

"Wait!" said the cat. "Here are some Fig Newtons." The Tookies hugged the boy and the cat. Then they got in the rocketship and blasted off. 10, 9, 8, 7, 6, 5, 4, 3, 2, 1, 0 . . . they were gone.

FIGURE 8–5   *Bill and the cat say good-bye to the Tookies*

of our extraordinary days together. The history that grew out of this time in our lives would become part of Jessie's "old story"—and would be forever engraved in our hearts.

Lingering Thoughts

When Brian and his family received word that they'd be moving to Missouri, they took a trip there to find a house. After they returned from their initial trip and it was definite that they were moving, Brian said to his mom, "I'd better call Mary Glover!" Brian called me to personally deliver his exciting family news. We had our conversation and then his mother and I talked. She said that even though Brian had been away from the school for a year, the ties were still very strong. I told her I felt the same way. I think we all did.

It's been a year and a half now since this class and I spent our last days together. A few of the children, like Brian, moved on to other schools, and I've only seen or heard from them through friends or an occasional card. Noah has been very faithful about remembering me on special holidays. (See Figure 9–1.)

After they left me, most of the children were in the classroom next door to mine and enjoyed a terrific year together. They adored their new teacher and loved being members of the oldest class in the school. For the most part we were all ready for a change. Since that time, I've had two new groups of students, both lively and endearing in their own way.

Although I've continued to grow as a teacher and still look forward to what each day will bring, my two-year class remains special. It was hard to let go of these children with whom I had built such a long history. I know my memory of them is selective; they appear in my mind as much more harmonious than they probably were in actuality.

It was, however, time for us to move on. Their year of learning with Yvonne, their new teacher, surpassed anything I could ever have done with them. They excelled in individual ways as well as a group. Maureen tackled seventh-grade algebra as a third grader, and Charlie successfully read Betsy Byar's *Summer of the Swans* after struggling the year before with the simplest of text. They needed someone besides me to help them up to the next step.

The separation from them with other classes in between has given me the time and the space to reflect on the various layers of meaning this time held for me, personally and as a teacher. I've been

FIGURE 9–1 *Noah's holiday card*

able to examine the experience more thoroughly to try to understand why the level of caring was so intense, why the letting go was such a painful process, and why the bonds of community were so strong. Several factors entered in.

A Matter of Timing

As I mentioned in the introduction, timing played a big part in setting the tone for these two years. I'd been out of the classroom for two years prior, and I was eager to get back to my work. I'd had time to reflect on what I believed and had extended my thinking in new ways in graduate school. I had also recently met Mary Ellen Giacobbe through a Center for Establishing Dialogue in Teaching and Learning

(CED) seminar. Her classroom demonstrations on the writing process were inspiring. My head was full of new ideas that I couldn't wait to try out with children. At the same time as I was being led back to the classroom, new and surprising possibilities began to arise for me as a writer.

An Emerging Author

For as long as I can remember, I've been a writer. When I was young I kept diaries filled with the private details of my inner world. I wrote poetry to try to sort out all the big questions about life and my existence. Letters to friends were an important part of my passage through adolescence. And there were, of course, all those meaningless papers and assignments required in school. As I grew into adulthood, I continued to keep a journal and write poetry, mostly to document historical events in my life. Writing was private—or at best meant to be shared with a limited number of people who knew me well. The thought of writing in a more public way never really crossed my mind. When two colleagues and I received notification that an article we'd written the summer before was to be published in *Language Arts*, this all changed. For the next two years, as I worked alongside this group of children, my professional writing entered a new dimension. The writing came forth like a whirlwind, playing an important role in the way in which theory and practice blended together in my classroom.

The most important writing for me was the year-long collaboration on the book with my friend Linda Sheppard (Glover & Sheppard, 1989). This was a process of examining daily classroom practice and then trying to interpret and express it in a form that would be accessible to others. That year of weekly writing sessions when Linda and I talked, laughed, and closely examined what we did each day in our classrooms, served the same purpose as a college seminar. Having someone consistently accessible for dialogue and support made the daily classroom work that much more rewarding and exciting. Our meetings not only helped us describe what we had done each week but they pushed our thinking about what the implications were for our children, ourselves, and classrooms beyond our own. Our sessions gave us a chance to try out ideas we received from each other— whether they were answers to problems or just ideas that had worked successfully in our classrooms. These conversations made us keenly aware of what was going on with our students. Because we knew what we were looking for, we were able to see more. As we noticed more, our dialogue became richer, and the writing evolved from there. This work with Linda, as well as additional summer writing with Yvonne Mersereau, gave me a unique opportunity to grow as a teacher who had become a writer. It brought a new element of fullness and intrigue to my classroom life.

Another situation also influenced my writing and, consequently, my work in the classroom. Through the efforts of our local teacher support group, I was fortunate to study with Donald Murray, a Pulitzer prize-winning author, for a month. For four Saturday mornings in a row, eleven other people and I sat with Don and talked about writing. We listened as he told of his own struggles as a writer and showed us examples of bits and pieces of work from his daybook. He shared copies of his *Boston Globe* column "Over Sixty." We read our own writing and felt validated as writers just by being in his presence.

The time with Don Murray had a lasting impression as I've continued my teaching and writing. It confirmed my belief in the power of writing. That understanding, that feeling of empowerment, is something I have been able to pass on to my students. My two-year class received the initial dose of that understanding. They were able to receive it because, in their own child ways, they knew how important it was to all of us. Those children came to know my love for writing and were able to pick up on my enthusiasm. In the process they took it on as their own.

When my writing describing them (Glover & Sheppard, 1989; Glover, 1990) was actually published, they were delighted to see their names in print. One morning late in the spring after our book had come out, I sat the class in a circle and handed them each an autographed copy. It was a rare moment. Some were absorbed in the text, sprawled in all sorts of reading postures, trying to follow every word. Other children bounced around excitedly making comments such as, "Hey, Mia! Here's your picture of the Japanese doll!" There was not only the thrill of seeing themselves represented in the book but also the understanding that even a writer they knew, their own teacher, had been published. Seeing their names, comments, and drawings in print was inspiring to this group of young writers. It helped them to see that what they do on a daily basis is important—to the point that others are interested in knowing more about it through the writing of their teacher.

Being both a writer and a teacher during this time brought a certain richness to my life, both professionally and personally. My writing, done with others and alone, allowed me to observe more closely the richness of my classroom life. It helped me to slow down and reflect. It stretched my ability to put into words that which had been thought but not expressed. The writing brought a sense of fulfillment as a teacher and as a person. Knowing that publication was possible, I wanted to do more. It made me work harder as a writer and as a teacher. My writing forced me to become a better listener and to pay closer attention to everything my students did. The writing served as a strong reminder that my students were also my teachers.

How Do You Get Your Ideas?

In first grade Jacob and I kept a dialogue journal. We'd write back and forth about a variety of topics. Our written conversations would range from discussions of his last summer's vacation to what his plans were for the coming weekend. During one series of conversations, we started exploring where authors and teachers get their ideas. I wrote that I often get my ideas from the children in the class, that I consider them to be my teachers. (See Jacob's response in Figure 9–2.)

His comment about getting ideas from when I write to him reinforced my faith in the power of writers and learners working together. When he wrote this, he reminded me how important other people are to us in the learning process. When we have others to help us along, we can go so much further in our thinking. This partnership also gives us access to a broader range of possibilities. The children were able to do this for me as well as for each other. They led me into territory as a teacher that I would never have anticipated. It was more than ideas for the classroom, however. The lessons they taught me affected the rest of my life too.

One of the greatest lessons I learned from these children was to not hold back any part of who I am as a person. They taught me to push the limits of what is possible and always stay close to the edge. It felt much the same as Anne Truitt's statement about artists: "The most demanding part of living a lifetime as an artist is the strict discipline of forcing oneself to work steadfastly along the nerve of one's own most intimate sensitivity" (Dillard, 1989, p. 68). The children gave me the inspiration and courage to stay in touch with that nerve; protecting it and, at the same time, always remaining alert to its potential for unexpected upheaval. It was a lesson in paying attention as much as a lesson in courage.

Other valuable teachings came through their laughter. The

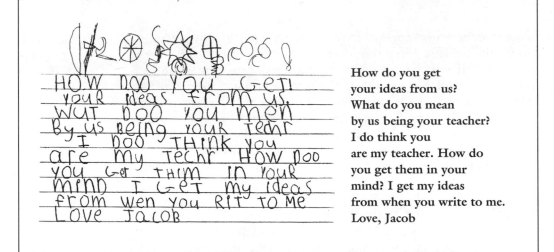

How do you get
your ideas from us?
What do you mean
by us being your teacher?
I do think you
are my teacher. How do
you get them in your
mind? I get my ideas
from when you write to me.
Love, Jacob

FIGURE 9–2 *Entry from Jacob's dialogue journal*

sense of humor that pervaded our classroom kept us all from taking anything, especially ourselves, too seriously. When tempers would flare or feelings were hurt, we could always count on laughter to set us straight again. Humor kept our classroom life healthy. On days when responsibilities or worries would start to drag me down, I could always depend on someone to come through with lines such as these:

MIA: My friend has a pig from Vietnam—they have dandruff, of course!

JESSICA: You have to use Perk shampoo to get it off!

BEN: Noah, do you like me to appreciate *your* ideas? Then you should appreciate mine!

JESSIE [AS SHE WAITS FOR ME TO PUT THE SPIRAL BINDING ON HER BOOK]: Mary, what color of a spinal are you going to put on my book?

BEN [NOTICING HIS PEN PAL DAVID'S NAME HAS TWO SYLLABLES]: Oh, my pen pal's name has two cylinders!

JESSICA (IN A DISCUSSION ABOUT THE DANGERS OF SMOKING): If someone came up to me and tried to give me some I'd just say, "Hey, Bozo, why don't you just smoke candy cigarettes or bubblegum cigarettes?"

CHARLIE [AFTER I HAVE GIVEN HIM SOME ASSISTANCE ON A MATH TEST AND REMAIN SITTING NEARBY HIM]: Uh, could I have a little privacy, please?

Their lively and humorous way of looking at the world affected my own perspective each day. When my thoughts would stray from the immediate situation, they would always bring me back to the moment through their delightful way of viewing the world and their playful approach to life. It was hard to stay too serious or preoccupied with other things when these comedians and entertainers were at work.

My Life Work

In *The Writing Life*, Annie Dillard (1989) writes:

> Push it. Examine all things intensely and relentlessly. Probe and search each object in a piece of art. Do not leave it, do not course over it, as if it were understood, but instead follow it down until you see it in the mystery of its own specificity and strength. (p. 78)

Although she was referring to writing, her words hold true for teaching as well. As I struggled to put into words what these two years and the children who were a part of them brought to me, Annie Dillard's lines struck a chord. The laughter, the inspiration for writing, the integration of work and play were all a part of it. But the heart of what they gave me was a sense of knowing what my life work is to be. I now realize that my life work will probably always include long teaching days in the classroom and evenings of planning and preparation. It will involve reflection through talk with others. It will be years of intense and relentless examining what happens in school and sharing these observations through writing. My life work will be watching and listening to children as I work to create a history with them.

I often think of the history these children and I shared. I remember the time when Maureen brought in her bag of human hair for our Japan study and the time we laughed hysterically when Denise wrote "How to Play Chees" instead of "Chess." I remember Brian's kindness to Charlie when he taught him how to play the money game, and the sadness everyone felt when Caitlin read her book about her dog running away. And how proud everyone was when Jenny told us about her pop fly. I think of the children each day as I glance at the collection of colorful plates that is now prominently displayed in my kitchen at home. I remember the colorfulness of the group and the richly textured history we composed together. I think of individuals, unique expressions of humanity, who stand on their own. But I remember them too as a collective group of children who, like the plates, were also part of a collection that as a whole became more than the sum of its parts. Although each one was exceptional in his or her own right, there was an element of strength in the collectiveness that surpassed what each member could be alone.

A year ago in late August, before the new school year was about to start, I received a phone call. On the other end of the line I heard a quivering voice ask, "Is Mary Glover there?" After identifying myself the voice replied, "This is Emily Thomas . . . from last year." Emily, the child who, on one of the first days of first grade, asked me if I was proud to be a teacher, had just finished her first day at her new school. She'd called to let me know she'd survived this major event. After a brief description of her social studies book, which she described as "kind of weird," her new best friend, whose name she could not remember, and her teacher who seemed nice, we agreed to talk again soon and said good-bye. I felt honored that Emily had called me to share this important news. I was touched by her reminder "from last year"—as if I'd ever forget her or any of her classmates! That small comment was her way of letting me know that those two years were important to her as well. And no matter how much time or space passed between any of us, there would always be a bond tying us together. A bond made of history and love.

A Circle
by Ben Hackbarth
A circle
full of love
holds each
other
If one happens to break
Allowing to flow out
The heart of the circle
Will be broken

References

Dillard, Annie. 1989. *The Writing Life*. New York: Harper & Row.

Glover, Mary Kenner. 1992. *Charlie's Ticket to Literacy*. Richmond Hill, Ontario: Scholastic-TAB Publications.

_____. 1990. "A Bag of Hair: American First Graders Experience Japan." *Childhood Education*, 66, 155–159.

Glover, Mary Kenner, and Sheppard, Linda. 1989. *Not on Your Own: The Power of Learning Together*. Richmond Hill, Ontario: Scholastic-TAB.

Greene, Maxine. 1978. *Landscapes of Learning*. New York: Teachers College Press.

Heard, Georgia. 1989. *For the Good of the Earth and the Sun*. Portsmouth, NH: Heinemann.

Kamii, Constance. 1989. *Young Children Continue to Reinvent Arithmetic*. New York: Teachers College Press.

Kohlberg, Lawrence, and Lickona, Thomas. 1987. "Moral Discussion and the Class Meeting." In *Constructivist Early Education: Overview and Comparison with Other Programs*, by Rheta DeVries with Lawrence Kohlberg. Washington, DC: National Association for the Education of Young Children.

Saint-Exupéry, Antoine de. 1943. *The Little Prince*. New York: Harcourt, Brace & World.

Smith, Frank. 1983. *Essays into Literacy*. Portsmouth, NH: Heinemann.

Wells, Gordon. 1986. *The Meaning Makers*. Portsmouth, NH: Heinemann.

Bibliography of Children's Literature

Allard, Harry. *Miss Nelson Is Missing*. New York: Scholastic, 1977.

_____. *The Stupids Step Out*. Boston: Houghton Mifflin, 1974.

Arbeit, Eleanor Werner. *Mrs. Cat Hides Something*. Layton, UT: Gibbs M. Smith, 1985.

Babbitt, Natalie. *Tuck Everlasting*. New York: Farrar, Straus & Giroux, 1975.

Browne, Anthony. *Willy the Wimp*. New York: Alfred A. Knopf, 1984.

Buck, Pearl S. *The Big Wave*. New York: Harper, 1947.

Burningham, John. *Come Away From the Water, Shirley*. New York: Crowell, 1977.

Byars, Betsy. *The Summer of the Swans*. New York: Viking, 1970.

dePaola, Tomie. *Tomie dePaola's Book of Poems*. New York: G. P. Putnam's Sons, 1988.

_____. *Nana Upstairs and Nana Downstairs*. New York: Putnam, 1973.

_____. *Now One Foot, Now the Other*. New York: Putnam, 1981.

Fox, Mem. *Wilfrid Gordon McDonald Partridge*. Brooklyn, NY: Kane/Miller, 1985.

George, Jean Craighead. *Julie of the Wolves*. New York: Harper & Row, 1972.

Greenfield, Eloise. *Grandmama's Joy*. New York: Philomel, 1980.

Handford, Martin. *Where's Waldo?* Boston: Little, Brown, 1987.

Howe, James. *Bunnicula*. New York: Atheneum, 1979.

Johnston, Tony. *Yonder*. New York: Scholastic, 1988.

Khalsa, Dayal Kaur. *Tales of a Gambling Grandma*. New York: Clarkson N. Potter, 1986.

Lobel, Arnold. *Frog and Toad All Year*. New York: Harper & Row, 1976.

Marshak, Samuil. *The Month Brothers*. New York: Morrow, 1983.

Marshall, Edward. *Fox in Love*. New York: Dial, 1982.

Martin, Bill, Jr. *Knots on a Counting Rope*. New York: Henry Holt, 1987.

MacLachlan, Patricia. *Sarah, Plain and Tall*. New York: Harper & Row, 1985.

Miller, Jonathan, and Pelham, David. *The Facts of Life*. New York: Viking, 1984.

Parker, Steve. *Skeleton*. New York: Alfred A. Knopf, 1988.

Prelutsky, Jack. *The New Kid on the Block*. New York: Greenwillow, 1984.

Rylant, Cynthia. *When I Was Young in the Mountains*. New York: E. P. Dutton, 1982.

Sendak, Maurice. *Where the Wild Things Are*. New York: Scholastic, 1983.

_____. *Outside Over There*. New York: Harper & Row, 1981.

Silverstein, Shel. *Where the Sidewalk Ends*. New York: Harper & Row, 1974.

Steig, William. *Dr. DeSoto*. New York: Scholastic, 1982.

_____. *Dominic*. New York: Farrar, Straus & Giroux, 1972.

_____. *Abel's Island*. New York, Farrar, Straus & Giroux, 1976.

Sterling, Dorothy. *Freedom Train*. Garden City, NY: Doubleday, 1954.

Sullivan, Charles (ed.). *Imaginary Gardens*. New York: Harry N. Abrams, 1989.

Van Allsburg, Chris. *Two Bad Ants*. Boston: Houghton Mifflin, 1988.

_____. *The Garden of Abdul Gasazi*. Boston: Houghton Mifflin, 1979.

_____. *Jumanji*. Boston: Houghton Miflin, 1981.

Walker, Alice. *To Hell with Dying*. New York: Harcourt Brace Jovanovich, 1988.

Whitfield, Philip and Whitfield, Ruth. *Why Do Our Bodies Stop Growing?* New York: Viking Kestrel, 1988.

Annotated Bibliography of Literature for Teachers

Ashton-Warner, Sylvia. *Teacher*. New York: Simon & Schuster, 1963.
    The first book I remember reading about teaching. It set the stage for the way I think about teaching and everything I do in the classroom.

Atwell, Nancie. *In the Middle: Writing, Reading, and Learning with Adolescents*. Portsmouth, NH: Boynton/Cook, 1987.
    Particularly helpful for middle- and upper-grade teachers.

Bazarini, Ronald. *Boys: A Schoolmaster's Journal*. New York: Walker, 1988.
    Delightfully written account of one teacher's classroom experience.

Bos, Bev. *Don't Move the Muffin Tins: A Hands-off Guide to Art for the Young Child*. Roseville, CA: Turn the Page Press, 1978.
    If I were to suggest one book on teaching children's art, this would be it.

Calkins, Lucy McCormick. *The Art of Teaching Writing*. Portsmouth, NH: Heinemann, 1986.
    An overview of the teaching of writing that was especially helpful for me when I was just beginning to establish a writing workshop.

————. *Living Between the Lines*. Portsmouth, NH: Heinemann, 1990.
    An inspiring reflection on ways to extend our thinking (and practice) about writing, and how to help children do the same.

Gentry, J. Richard. *Spel . . . Is a Four-Letter Word*. Portsmouth, NH: Heinemann, 1987.
>   An important book about invented spelling and related issues.

Goodman, Kenneth S. *What's Whole in Whole Language?*. Portsmouth, NH: Heinemann, 1986.
>   A brief overview of whole language theory and practice. A good book for parents who have questions.

Graves, Donald. *Writing: Teachers and Children at Work*. Portsmouth, NH: Heinemann, 1983.
>   The first book I read on writing process. Among other things, it covers how to get children started with writing, how to conduct conferences and keep records. This book changed my teaching life.

Greene, Maxine. *Landscapes of Learning*. New York: Teachers College Press, 1978.
>   A food-for-thought book which I frequently return to for a deeper look at things. Thoughtfully examines social issues related to teaching, aesthetics, and wide-awakeness in education and women in education.

Heard, Georgia. *For the Good of the Earth and Sun: Teaching Poetry*. Portsmouth, NH: Heinemann, 1989.
>   The best book I know on teaching poetry to children. It is a wonderful blend of sensitive reflections on poetry and practical know-how for teaching poetry in the classroom.

Kamii, Constance. *Children Continue to Reinvent Arithmetic*. New York: Teachers College Press, 1989.
>   Explanation of constructivist theory and how to apply it mathematically. This book has profoundly altered the way I teach math.

Mayeroff, Milton. *On Caring*. New York: Harper & Row, 1971.
>   A thoughtful book on the important subject of caring. Examines how qualitites such as patience, hope, and honesty contribute to our relationships with others.

Mearns, Hughes. *Creative Power*. New York: Doubleday, 1929. Reprint. New York: Dover, 1958.
>   Written by one of John Dewey's contemporaries, this is a timeless book about creativity and how to foster it in children.

Murray, Donald M.. *Expecting the Unexpected: Teaching Myself—and Others—to Read and Write*. Portsmouth, NH: Boynton/Cook, 1989.
>   A collection of articles about writing (and teaching) by one of

the most influential people in my writing life. Includes thoughts on how to write badly to write well, overcoming writer's block, and sitting to write.

Newman, Judith M. *Whole Language: Theory in Use.* Portsmouth, NH: Heinemann, 1985.

Covers a variety of whole language issues including invented spelling. Introductory chapters give one of the most thorough and accessible explanations of whole language I've read.

Paley, Vivian. *Wally's Stories.* Cambridge, MA: Harvard University Press, 1981.

One of several books by a teacher who knows how to listen to children.

Peterson, Ralph, and Eeds, Maryann. *Grand Conversations.* Richmond Hill, Ontario: Scholastic-TAB, 1990.

A complete overview of literature study that includes theory as well as practical applications.

Smith, Frank. *Insult to Intelligence.* New York: Arbor House, 1986.

An important book for anyone involved in school policy and curriculum development.

van Manen, Max. *The Tone of Teaching.* Portsmouth, NH: Heinemann, 1986.

A reflection on pedagogy that I think should be required reading by all educators and teachers in training.

Wells, Gordon. *The Meaning Makers: Children Learning Language and Using Language to Learn.* Portsmouth, NH: Heinemann, 1986.

An excellent study of children's early language and literacy learning. Helpful in explaining whole language learning model to parents.